WHAT DOGS HEAR

UNDERSTANDING CANINE HEARING AND BEHAVIOR
FROM PUPPY TO SENIOR

JANET MARLOW, M.A., SOUND BEHAVIORIST

 **Pet Acoustics**

What Dogs Hear © 2020 Pet Acoustics, Inc.

All rights reserved. No part of this publication may be reproduced, stored in a retrieval system, or transmitted, in any form by any means, electronic, mechanical, photocopying, recording, or otherwise without prior permission from the publisher.

Layout by www.formatting4U.com

Contributors-
The Editorial Department- Jonathan Balcombe, Editorial Guidance
Tessera Editorial- Ronni Davis, Editor

Special Photo Credits
Julian Kirschner, Laura Stanley, Albina Chamonixdeus, Will Osborne, Teresa Berg, Dominika Roseclay, Nikolay Tchaouchev, Cheryl Martinelli

Pet Acoustics, Inc.
P.O. Box 26
Washington Depot, CT 06794
Website: PetAcoustics.com
Contact: hello@petacoustics.com
+1-860-459-8000

ISBN: 978-0-578-76446-7

For Rigby

IN GRATITUDE TO:

Jonathan Balcombe, scientist, author and advisor; Henry E. Heffner and Rickye S. Heffner, researchers; Ronni Davis, Editor; Judi Fennell of formatting4U.com; Nikoo McGoldrick, author and advisor; Cheryl Martinelli, photo contributions; Will Osborne, the staff at Litchfield Veterinary Hospital, Lori McClain-Russak of the Fidelco Guide Dog Foundation; Lu and Dale Picard, founders of Educated Canines Assisting with Disabilities; Rachel McPherson, founder of The Good Dog Foundation; Kristina Spaulding, Ph.D.; Northshore Animal League; The Little Guild; Operation Freedom Paws; Danbury Animal Welfare Society; my family and my husband Alan Brennan.

WHAT THE DOG PERHAPS HEARS

If an inaudible whistle
blown between our lips
can send him home to us,
then silence is perhaps
the sound of spiders breathing
and roots mining the earth;
it may be asparagus heaving,
headfirst, into the light
and the long brown sound
of cracked cups, when it happens.

We would like to ask the dog
if there is a continuous whir
because the child in the house
keeps growing, if the snake
really stretches full length
without a click and the sun
breaks through clouds without
a decibel of effort,
whether in autumn, when the trees
dry up their wells, there isn't a shudder
too high for us to hear.

What is it like up there?
above the shut-off level
of our simple ears?
For us there was no birth cry,
the newborn bird is suddenly here,
the egg broken, the nest alive,
and we heard nothing when the world changed.

Lisel Mueller
Pulitzer *Winning Poet*
(1924-2020)

This book is dedicated to my dear friend, Mary Pope Osborne, whose illumination of life and love of dogs is always a delight.

CONTENTS

PREFACE: The Modern Dog i
INTRODUCTION: The Agreement v
CHAPTER 1: How Ears Detect and Process Sound 1
CHAPTER 2: What We Hear, What They Hear 7
CHAPTER 3: Ear Shape and Breed Purpose. It's Complicated! 15
CHAPTER 4: Discovery and Human Perspective 21
CHAPTER 5: The Psychology of Hearing 27
CHAPTER 6: Hearing Health—Puppy to Senior 37
CHAPTER 7: Using Technology to See Sound 45
CHAPTER 8: Test Your Dog's Hearing 51
CHAPTER 9: Classical Music, TV, Radio. What Works? 55
CHAPTER 10: Thunderstorms and Fireworks 61
CHAPTER 11: The Pitch of Your Voice 69
CHAPTER 12: Mitigating Sound Stress in Shelters, Kennels, Homes, Veterinary Hospitals, and Training Environments 79
CHAPTER 13: Rhythms for 10,000 Walks 89
CHAPTER 14: The Invention of Species-Specific Music 95
CHAPTER 15: Follow the Dog 101
ABOUT JANET MARLOW 103
ABOUT PET ACOUSTICS 105
INDEX 108
RESEARCH REFERENCES 109

PREFACE:

The Modern Dog

As twenty-first century pet parents, we are part of a new era of pet care, one that recognizes dogs as cognitive beings. Think about it. More than fifty years ago—if dogs were lucky—they slept outside in a doghouse and ate the scraps from dinner table meals. Today, with dogs in our good care, a species evolution is occurring.

How is this happening? The modern dog travels in our cars often strapped in for safety, he travels on trains and subways, and he gets his own reserved seat on airplanes. Dogs have appointments to be bathed, groomed, and styled. Our dogs get veterinary health check-ups and undergo cutting-edge medical surgeries with human-grade post-op care. Dogs are taken to daycare and socialized at the dog park. They're taking agility course training, enjoying daily walks and athletic runs, and having playdates with their own circle of canine friends whose names, when spoken, are acknowledged with enthusiastic tail wags. Sometimes, it seems like the only things a modern dog lacks are a driver's license and a mobile phone!

These physical and mental stimulations in our modern dog's daily life elicit a conscious willingness from your dog. Today, our canine companions are light-years beyond their origins of purpose for survival.

Our human empathy toward our dogs has evolved because of this new level of relationship. When we're not with our dogs, we

What Dogs Hear

use technological devices to provide daily care. For example, instead of just a bowl, we now use time-released feeders with perfectly portioned food. Pet camera devices installed in our homes can dispense a treat triggered from an app on our smartphones when we feel an emotional pang of missing our dog while away from them. Some pet parents can take their fur baby to work with them, where the dog can rest on a comfortable dog bed while he listens to canine-calming music, which soothes him while the office bustles around him. Dogs have visits from a pet sitter for human contact and walks to maintain their daily schedule. In all, they are members of our families and cared for as such, and this level of canine life is an evolution that is happening globally.

Scientists have long studied the close relationship between humans and dogs, and various theories have been proposed to explain just how far back in time the relationship goes. Most agree that dogs and humans have coexisted for at least 16,000 years. Canines have served in partnership with humans as hunting dogs, guard dogs, and herding dogs. Today, pet parents, veterinarians, and behaviorists are becoming more aware that a balanced life for a dog is more complex than just those original purposes. Being part of this new era to help the modern dog adapt to their new pace of life is a dedication that I committed to in 1994.

The founder of Green Chimneys, Dr. Samuel B. Ross, wisely said to me, "One animal can change a life!" Dr. Ross was right! At that time, I was focusing on my career as an international performer and recording artist in jazz and classical music. When I was home practicing for performances, I was always delighted that, no matter where my dogs or cats were in the house, they would come to my side, curl up, and rest deeply, listening to my classical guitar playing and jazz singing. One day, my beloved black-and-white cat, Osborn, went missing and was later found wounded. I rushed him to our local veterinarian hospital where, for five days, I sang to him while he was in the ICU. I could tell by the way he blinked his eyes slowly that he was being soothed by my soft singing. Sadly, my dear Osborn passed away. He was fifteen years old. Days later, I could not stop asking myself questions. Why are animals so profoundly affected by music? What is it about their hearing that brings them to certain sounds, and, conversely, why do they flee from certain sounds? My head was spinning as I grieved, and, in those days of deep thought, I committed the rest of my life to discovering the answers.

Over the next three years, I sought out research from universities on animal hearing. I received studies from researchers to understand this new field of science. From cows to bats, I learned the phenomenal range of hearing abilities that nature has given our fellow beings, including dogs and cats.

As a composer with my own recording studio, I started formulating music concepts with a new approach, different from the recording techniques I had learned for human hearing. The question was that if my dogs and cats were soothed by music, how could I make that experience measurable and repeatable for the well-being for other people's dogs and cats? I soon developed a composing technique using sustaining instruments while digitally modifying the spectrum of sounds according to the data of each animal's hearing range. The goal was to provide an animal with a specific music environment based on their hearing comfort range using frequencies and decibels that would consistently calm behavior. I created hours of music that became a formula I could apply to any composition. I spent the next year giving the music to veterinarians, kennels, shelters, and pet parents to try. The responses were extremely positive!

"Pet Acoustics' music for dogs and cats has a significant calming effect on our hospitalized patients. We have found it helps to reduce their anxiety while away from their families."—Litchfield Veterinary Hospital.

"No more stress and anxiety. Starts working quickly. Who'd have thought that a little music could soothe a stressed-out pet?" a pet parent responded.

What Dogs Hear

In 1997, I solidified the digital composing process of producing species-specific music for dogs, cats, horses, and birds. Twenty-six years later, my approach to music for animals has been clinically proven, with studies published in veterinary science journals, and has helped thousands of pet parents with their pets' behavior.

As I talked to more and more pet parents and veterinarians, I learned that the sonic environment was an overlooked reason for stress behaviors in dogs. These caregivers shared observations of their dogs, describing terrorized responses to thunderstorm and firework events, excessive barking triggered by sounds in the home, lunging at the sound of car wheels or high frequency bicycle spokes speeding down the street, and intense ground vibrations causing some dogs to jump into a bathtub to get a sense of safety. Where do these responses come from? How could pet parents help their dogs mitigate sound stress? How could veterinarians modify their sonic environment so dogs could have less fearful visits?

The following chapters in this book are an invitation to learn more about your relationship with your dog and your dog's relationship to their world through their amazing ears. You'll learn about the science of sound and how it affects canine behavior. Explore their phenomenal hearing ability and how to resolve behavioral issues throughout each stage of your dog's life.

INTRODUCTION:

The Agreement

I've brought many animals into my home, embracing each one as a beloved member of my family. Inevitably, within a short period of time, I would come to the same conclusion: an agreement had been formed between me and my new fur-family member. Living together, daily tugs and pulls of expectations unfold not just over play toys, but over an interspecies exchange of wills. This tension is understandable from our human perspective since we ask our fellow animals to live in our world as if it should be natural to them. In time, however, a daily rhythmic flow for rest, activity, feeding, and playtime fits into our human schedules. A threshold of trust is developed and the relationship agreement is established.

With many good people adopting from shelters these days, it's not always a smooth transition into the agreement. Rescue dogs more often than not have a negative start in life for varying reasons, which is likely unknowable to the adopter. Behaviors can be resistant in response to expectations and training until your dog understands she is safe. In time, with patience and care, a new agreement can be formed to dissipate negative memories and move into a happier life.

Listening to your dog and your dog listening to you is essential for a good relationship. Vocal communication, environmental sounds, and canine acute hearing are important areas of interaction and caregiving. For example, there is a store in my town that Rigby, my English Springer Spaniel, and I walk by every day. Being a dog-friendly store, the owner loves to see dogs and gives them treats at the counter. When we walk by and the store is closed, Rigby immediately pulls me, leash-in-hand, up to the door. I stand there, making the case out loud like a courtroom lawyer, "I'm sorry, Rigby, the store is closed and we can't go in today." He hears me and looks at the door just in case I've forgotten how to go in. I can see his doggy brain saying, "Is she going to open the door? The treats are in there! What's the hold up?" I see his disappointed eyes still mulling over the situation. I repeat softly, "I'm sorry, Rigby, the store is closed, and we can't go in today. Perhaps another time." He finally shows acceptance and moves away from the door, then we continue our walk. You may ask why I didn't just pull the leash and collar to make him move. In this scenario, pulling on the leash doesn't allow time for him to become cognitive and give him choice. Rigby has been trained by me to respond to verbal communication for direction, which has created a positive relationship in our six-year agreement. You'll see in many chapters in this book that I focus on tools and techniques to enhance communication through mutual listening.

Throughout the human-canine relationship, sound as a stimulus and as a communication tool is often overlooked as a cause-and-effect of different canine behaviors. Canine acute hearing is often attributed to behaviors such as stress, anxiety, aggression, and fear. As their caregivers, we also need to know our own hearing abilities in order to recognize their needs and sound communication. Do you hear the highest frequencies and whines uttered by your dog? Have you noticed your dog's hearing diminishing in response to you now that he is a senior? Do you know how to mitigate your home environment to minimize stress reactivity during thunderstorm and firework events? As a researcher on canine hearing and as an inventor of solutions for canine stress triggered by sound, I am writing this book as my agreement with you to help you know your dog through their amazing hearing ability and what this means for their well-being. Each chapter is sequenced to unfold these important aspects that can be used as tools and techniques to enhance the quality of your dog's life and bring your relationship to a deeper level of communication with continued love and bonding.

CHAPTER 1:

How Ears Detect and Process Sound

(what sound is, the structure and function of mammalian ears, and how they process sound)

To begin understanding your dog's hearing world, we look to the science of sound, which the biology of humans and animals share. Sound moves through air, which gives rise to vibrations that travel and can be heard when they reach a person's or animal's ear.

The anatomy and the physiology of the human ear is similar in structure and function to the canine ear. The human ear's function is to transmit and transduce sound to the brain through the outer ear, the middle ear, and the inner ear.

Human Ear Anatomy

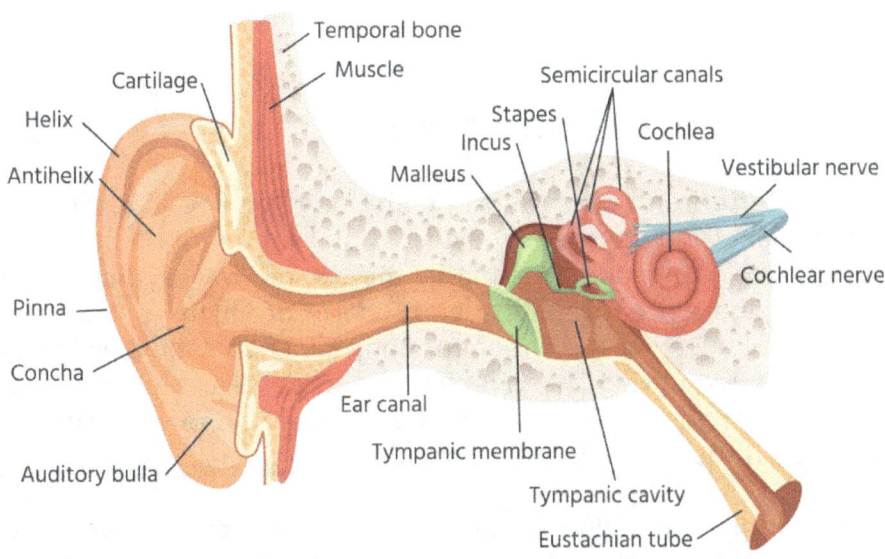

Both human and canine ears have an outer ear (pinna), middle ear (Tympanic membrane) and an inner ear (cochlea).

Canine Ear Anatomy

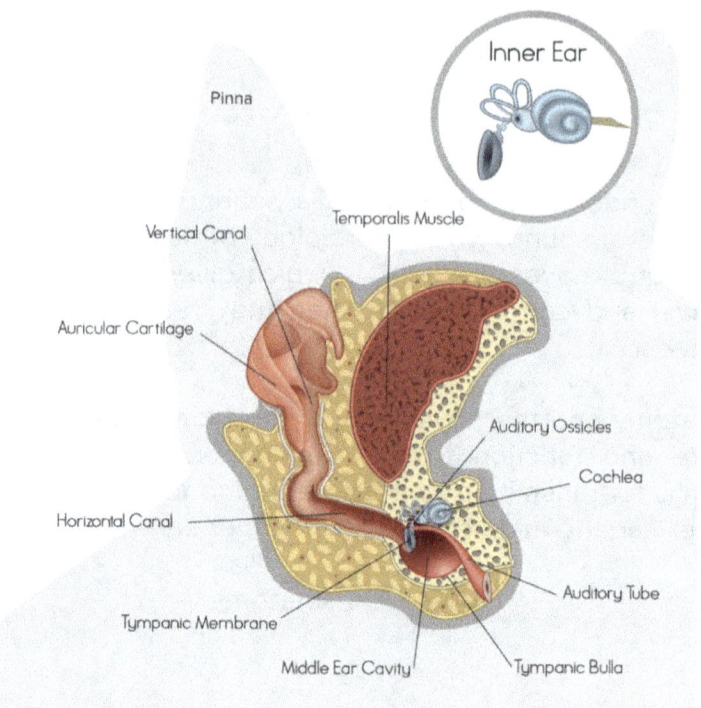

The Canine Ear

The **outer ear** includes the pinna (the part you see that is made of cartilage and covered by skin, fur or hair) and the ear canal. The pinna is shaped to capture the sound waves that travel through the ear canal to the eardrum. In dogs, the pinnae are mobile and can move independently of each other, which is good for identifying the directional source of the sound. The size and shape of the pinnae vary by breed. The ear canal of the dog is much deeper than the human ear canal.

The **middle ear** includes the eardrum or Tympanic membrane and a small, air-filled chamber that contains three tiny bones: the hammer, anvil, and stirrup, just like the human ear. It also includes two muscles: the oval window (a membrane covering the entrance to the cochlea in the inner ear) and the Eustachian tube (a narrow tube that connects the middle ear with the back of the nose, allowing air to enter the middle ear).

The **inner ear** is a complex structure that includes the cochlea (the organ of hearing) and the vestibular system (the organ of balance).

Sound is a physical phenomenon that is scientifically described as decibels (volume) and frequencies (pitch). The invisible air that surrounds us is a conduit for sound. Because sound is invisible, humans don't realize that their mood or sense of agitation may be highly affected by sound. The conclusion of a study from the Ludwig Maximilian University in Munich, Germany and published in *Royal Society Open Science*, shows that being exposed to inaudible sounds for only ninety seconds can have an effect on the inner ear, such as exposure to infrasonic sounds. Infrasonic sounds are under 20 Hz, too low for the human ear to detect. Additionally, the human ear can experience noise-induced hearing loss (NIHL), one of the most common auditory pathologies, resulting from overstimulation of the cochlea. Hearing loss occurs in canines as well when exposed to loud noises. Inside the cochlea, there are thousands of tiny hair cells. Hair cells change the vibrations into electrical signals that are sent to the brain through the hearing nerve. Each hair cell has a small patch of stereocilia sticking up out of the top of it. When these hairs flatten over time due to air pressure from loud noises, hearing loss follows.

The good news is that your dog has phenomenal hearing. The acoustic environment in which your dogs are hearing is a great barometer of why they behave the way they do.

The term *acoustics* is defined by Oxford Languages as "properties or qualities of a room or building that determine how sound is transmitted within it." Auditory perception (hearing) is the ability to perceive sounds by detecting vibrations and changes in air pressure through the ear.

The canine ear has twice the frequency range of humans. Even

What Dogs Hear

though dogs hear more than we do from puppy to adult, their hearing ability diminishes as they age to senior, the same way humans experience hearing loss as we age. Knowing the science of your dog's hearing function and ability is as important to a healthy life as much as giving them the best nutrition and exercise.

You may have done a canine head-tilt when you read the term *sound behaviorist* on the cover of this book. Sound behavior is a new term for the study in which an animal or person acts in response to a particular situation or stimulus from sound. A sound behaviorist is a person who specializes in the study of behavior in response to auditory perception and acoustics.

The science and research on the effects of sound has led to great progress and invention in our modern world. Sound is measured in decibels and frequencies. Historically, the measurement of a decibel was invented by Alexander Graham Bell (1847-1922), who was also the inventor of the telephone, decades before the smartphone. The first part of the word (deci) means *ten*—for ten cycles of sound. The second half of the word is *bel*, named after Mr. Bell. The symbol for the word *decibel* is dB, which represents the measurement of volume. It is a relative unit of measurement, corresponding to one-tenth of a bel. It is used to express the ratio of one value of a power or field quantity to another on a logarithmic scale.

For reference, here are examples of sounds with their corresponding dB levels.

Noise Source	Decibel Level
Thunderclap, chain saw (121 dB).	120
Live rock music (108 - 114 dB).	110
Power mower (96 dB); motorcycle at 25 ft (90 dB).	90
Food blender (88 dB); garbage disposal (80 dB).	80
Passenger car at 65 mph (77 dB); Living room music (76 dB); radio or TV-audio, vacuum cleaner (70 to 80dB).	70

Conversation in restaurant, office, background music	60
Quiet suburb, conversation at home	50
Library, bird calls (44 dB)	40
Quiet rural area	30
Whisper, rustling leaves	20
Breathing	10
Threshold of human hearing	0

The second category of sound is known as *frequency*. Frequency is also called *pitch*. A bass drum reverberation, rumbling thunder, and a deep voice are low-frequency sounds. A high-pitched whistle, a squeak or a young child's voice are examples of high-frequency sounds.

The German physicist, Heinrich Hertz (1857-1894), discovered how to measure pitch or frequency. A Hertz (Hz) is a unit of frequency (one cycle of sound per second), the rate at which a vibration occurs that constitutes a wave, either in a material (as in sound waves) or in an electromagnetic field (as in radio waves and light).

Now that you know that sound can be measured by decibels (dB) and frequencies (Hz), we begin our journey to better understand why this invisible world of sound matters for human and canine well-being. The spectrum of dB and Hz experienced in our daily living environment can be the cause of positive and negative behaviors. If you've observed a dog during an intense thunderstorm or while a series of fireworks is exploding nearby, stress and anxiety in response to these sounds are very apparent. There are, however, many levels of frequencies and decibels in the air that we can't hear that are the direct cause of a dog's behavior—positive or negative. By the time you have read this book, it is my hope that you will become astutely aware of the world of sound for your dog's well-being.

Let's start where you and your dog are right now in this space and time. Did you know that the Earth emits its own frequency?

What Dogs Hear

Did you know this benefits your dog?

In 1954, H.L. König confirmed the physicist Otto Schumann's hypothesis, detecting Earth's resonance at a frequency of 7.83 Hz—known as the *Schumann Resonance*. This was established by measuring global electromagnetic resonances generated and excited by lightning discharges in the ionosphere. The importance is that it acts as a background frequency, influencing the biological circuitry of the mammalian brain. "You can think of this as the Earth's heartbeat," as described by Dr. Joe Dispenza, international lecturer and researcher.

How do these standing waves, known as the Schumann Resonance, affect your beloved dog? If your dog spends time walking in the grass, he receives a boost of energy from the Earth through his paws. Have you seen your dog lie in the grass, calm and content? He knows instinctively that he is getting energy from the Earth.

Let's look further into how sound affects your dog.

CHAPTER 2:

What We Hear, What They Hear

(a comparative discussion of dog and human hearing abilities)

The frequency chart below illustrates how other species' hearing compares to humans'.

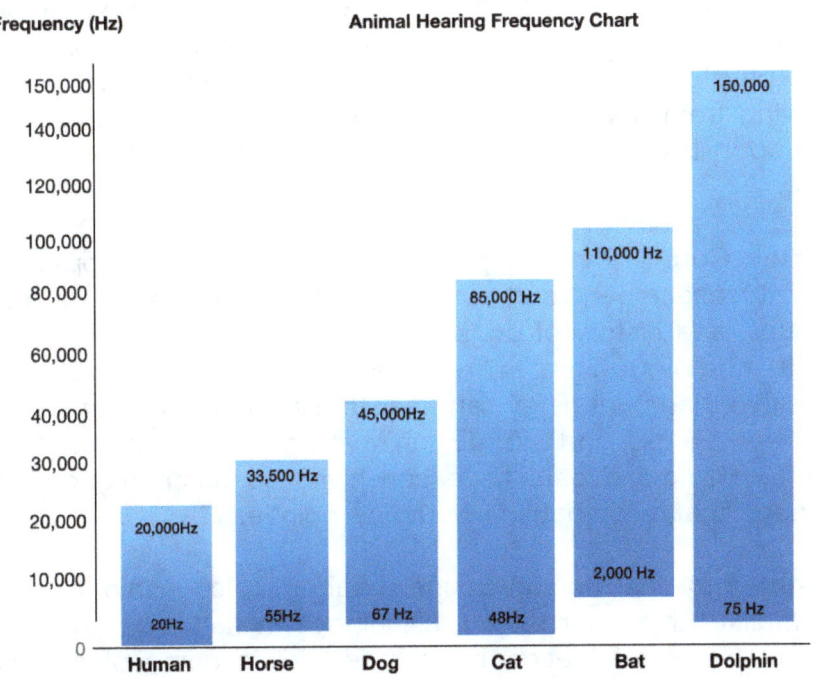

It's clear that dogs hear twice as much as humans while cats hear three times more than humans. Horses and humans have the most closely related hearing range of any comparative mammals.

Looking further into human hearing is a good place to start understanding your dog's amazing ears! The lowest frequency a human can hear is 20 Hz. Any sounds lower than 20 Hz are felt as vibrations, such as the rumbling during an earthquake.

What Dogs Hear

Infants' frequency range is between 20 Hz to 20,000 Hz. The highest frequency range a young person can hear is between 12,000 Hz to 16,000 Hz. Over 60 years of age, the upper hearing range diminishes from a range of 2,000 Hz to 8,000 Hz. The point being that, as we age, our ability to hear upper register sounds becomes less and less.

Juxtaposed to humans, a healthy dog hears from 67 Hz to 45,000 Hz. As dogs age, they will experience hearing loss as well. Very often, an aging dog will have lost some ability to hear without the pet parent being aware of this until a veterinary checkup reveals the hearing loss. It is common among dogs to hide physical vulnerabilities or show pain, which is an instinct deriving from pack survival. Over time, a dog will increasingly rely upon his sight and smell to compensate for any hearing loss.

Stanley Coren, Ph.D., a psychology professor, neuropsychological researcher, and writer on the intelligence, mental abilities, and history of dogs says, "When sounds are between 3,000 and 12,000 Hz in frequency, dogs' ears are far more sensitive than ours. They can hear those sounds when they are between -5 dB and -15 dB on average. For sounds above 12,000 Hz, dogs' ears have sensitivity so much higher than humans' that a comparison would be pointless."

Insight into the human-canine hearing relationship can be exemplified by other biological pairings in nature in regard to sound. Have you heard the phrase, "It's a game of cat-and-mouse"? Cats are good mice hunters because they can hear the high squeaks and movements that mice produce. In return, a mouse can easily detect the cat approaching because mice hear up to 91,000 Hz, almost equal to the feline hearing level of 85,000 Hz.

Another example of similar hearing acuity is the mosquito and the bat. The buzzing sound of mosquitoes is caused by the vibration of their wings, referred to as a *flight tone*. Bats hear from 2,000 Hz to 110,000 Hz. Bats have a concentration of receptor cells in their inner ear, making them extremely sensitive to frequency changes. Bats also use *echolocation* to detect insect prey by passively listening to sounds emanating from the insects themselves. Mosquitoes, as a defense, can sense a bat from a hundred feet away. This is nature's interspecies hearing game.

Even though we are living together, when sounds go above 20,000 Hz, only our dogs can experience these levels. For example, you know your hearing limitations when your dog runs to the window barking, but you look outside and can't see or hear the cause of the barking. Your dog is definitely telling you he hears something out there. If you want to get an immediate sensation of enhanced canine hearing, cup your ears forward using your hands. This mimics the dog's funnel ear shape, which heightens the sound waves and will give you a wider capture of sound.

Let's now talk about how volume (dB)—or loudness of sound—can affect your dog. According to the research of Henry E. Heffner and Rickye S. Heffner at the University of Toledo Laboratory of Animal Comparative Hearing, a dog's volume comfort level is between 60 dB and 80 dB. This happens to be the same volume comfort levels for humans as well.

Human and dogs share the same hearing comfort range: 60 dB to 80 dB

What Dogs Hear

The intensity of volume, measured in decibels, greatly affects canine behavior. If you have lived with a dog, you probably know that turning on a vacuum cleaner can cause your dog to run away or bark at the machine in agitation. This is because a vacuum cleaner emits high frequency whines which we can't hear, causing pressure in the dog's inner ear.

Any sound source that causes intense pressure in a dog's ear can eventually alter the physical function of the ear. Located just before the cochlea in the inner ear are small fibers called cilia hairs. If sounds are excessive, the cilia—which is upright—no longer rebounds to this normal position. For a dog, this is felt as pressure or pain which can trigger behavioral stress. Over time, if there is consistent exposure to intense noise, the cilia will eventually remain damaged and hearing loss will occur. Sustained sounds above a dog's comfort volume level are detrimental to canine hearing health. It is important for pet parents to know and identify volume levels, as we should always remove a dog from an excessively loud environment for these reasons.

Have you noticed that your dog can hear the arrival of a person to your home before you do? A dog's hearing enables him to detect sounds up to four times farther than we can. Dogs' sound-response reflex is much faster than most humans, too. Because their ears can move independently, dogs can locate, isolate, and react to a sound in 0.06 of a second. A sound you are able to hear from twenty yards away would be audible to a dog from a distance of eighty yards. Moveable ears allow dogs to pinpoint sounds within that range. The value of knowing your dog's hearing capability is a key insight into the subtleties of why dogs behave the way they do.

Canine behavior can be categorized in three zones of hearing reactivity. This chart shows the frequency ranges which trigger each level: Balanced, Environmental, and Acute.

What Dogs Hear

Canine Hearing Stress Zones

Balanced Behavior **Environmental Stress** **Acute Stress**

3,000 Hz -12,000Hz   12,000 Hz -25,000Hz   25,000Hz and above

Knowing the frequency content of your dog's hearing environment can help you predict canine behavior. Later, in Chapter Seven, I will show you how technology can help you determine these Hz levels.

Balanced Behavior: If the frequency content in the environment is between 3,000 Hz-12,000 Hz, your dog's behavior will generally be in a state of balance with the environment. They will be calm and show a sense of safety and confidence.

Environmental Stress: If the frequency content in the environment is between 12,000 Hz -25,000 Hz, your dog can show the following behaviors: startled movements, anxious barking, shedding, agitation, and a state of hypervigilance. Hypervigilance as a behavior can also be a physical signal to communicate to a pack that there is danger. These are warning signs of environmental stress.

Acute Stress: If the frequency content in your dog's environment is 25,000Hz and above, your dog will be in acute stress, with behaviors, such as trembling, panting, pacing, drooling, hyper-salivation, fear, aggression, cowering, and hiding.

Even though your hearing is not accessing most of these frequencies, you can trust that the reactive behavior your dog is showing is in response to what's happening in the environment.

What Dogs Hear

Dogs are like a barometer indicating what is occurring in the air in regard to frequency levels.

Dogs respond accordingly, either moving toward or away from sound. If you're reading this book, you may already be aware of stress issues having observed them in your own pup or from hearing about these issues from friends. Hypervigilance is a behavioral response to sound which can manifest physically as trembling, hypersalivation, hiding, escaping, barking, and whining. When dogs are in this state in the wild, they can flee from the agitating sounds. This instinctual behavior remains active in our domesticated dogs, but the difference between living in the wild and living in modern indoor life is that there is minimal space for dogs to distance themselves from the agitating sound source. In our homes, shelters or veterinary practices, sound is an invisible trigger of behavior. There are things that we can do as caregivers to mitigate sound stress in these environments.

CHAPTER 3:

Ear Shape and Breed Purpose. It's Complicated!

The size and shape of a dog's ear, as well as the dog's breed, determines how their ears capture sound. Hound and Beagle breeds have the benefit of drop-shaped ears, which capture scents for the benefit of tracking and hunting. Shepherd breeds have upright ears and are able to detect the faintest of sounds in the distance, often working alongside humans in rescue and recovery missions. Sheepdogs can hear a predator or other danger approaching and can quickly herd the sheep to safety.

There are 18 muscles in a dog's ear which gives them the ability to move them independently. They can change their ear position to capture sound whether close or distant. Ear position is also an expression of their emotion. For example, ears facing forward means they are paying close attention or being curious. Ears flat against the head means fear or aggression. Ears slightly back can mean feeling sad. A head tilt can mean a dog is tuning into a distant sound. Ear direction along with body positioning are indicators of emotions.

There are 12 Breed Shapes of Canine Ears

- Prick Ears (German Shepherds)
- Candle Flame Ears (Dobermans)
- Blunt-Tipped Ears (French Bulldogs)
- Bat Ears (Chihuahuas)
- Hooded Ears (Basenjis)
- Cocked Ears (Collies)
- Drop Ears (Hounds)
- Button Ears (Jack Russells)
- Rose Ears (Bulldogs)
- Folded Ears (Spaniels)
- V-Shaped Ears (Vizslas)
- Filbert-Shaped Ears (Bedlington Terriers)

What Dogs Hear

In years past, you could rely on the identification of the shape of the ear to determine canine purpose, like the purebred Border Collie with his perked ears and strong instinct to herd. In the twenty-first century, determining dog purpose according to ear shape is more complicated due to cross breeding and designer husbandry. The practice of husbandry has and continues to alter the natural physical traits of recognized common breeds. Charles Darwin, the English naturalist, geologist, and biologist, called this *domestication syndrome*. This means that, with all good intentions, the breeding process results in biological variables. For example, instead of an upright ear, the ear structure of a dog becomes weak and, through generational breeding, the floppy ear becomes an unexpected surprise and then a consistent trait over time. Due to the accentuation of certain breed characteristics, negative traits have resulted, such as breathing difficulties in Bulldogs and hip dysplasia in German Shepherds.

Another complication with determining purpose and ear shape is the practice of ear cropping, which is often perceived as a health benefit and also done for cosmetic reasons. There is, however, no data to support that cropping a dog's ears improves its health. Ear cropping means cutting off the floppy part of a dog's ear. The procedure is performed, with anesthesia, on dogs when they are between the ages of six- and twelve-weeks-old. The ears are then taped to a hard surface for several weeks while they heal so they stay upright, as commonly done on Dobermans. The American Kennel Club (AKC) says the practices are "integral to defining and preserving breed character." I would also like to make note that The American Veterinary Medical Association (AVMA) opposes docking and cropping. "The most common reason for cropping and docking is to give a dog a certain look. That means it poses unnecessary risks," says Emily Patterson-Kane, PhD at the AVMA Animal Welfare Division.

If your dog is a combination of breeds, their ear shape may not correspond to their body type, which can be tested with a DNA kit. There are many types of kits available, and the test will reveal the combination of your mixed breed dog. Additionally, the results of the DNA testing may provide clues to your dog's behavioral traits and quirks, and even help identify breed-specific health problems.

What Dogs Hear

Though the shape of the ear is highly variable among different dogs, they do share the commonality of hearing responses as a specie to frequencies and decibels. The study by Henry E. Heffner, Hearing in Large and Small Dogs: Absolute Thresholds and Size of the Tympanic Membrane, Heffner states, "From the present results, it appears that, in the latter sense of the term, there is no obvious correlation among dogs between the size of a dog or the size of its tympanum and its auditory sensitivity."

Canine ears with their acute hearing will always give us clues as to their behavior.

CHAPTER 4:

Discovery and Human Perspective

I truly believe that much of what we are now uncovering about animal life and behavior stems from our human consciousness expanding to embrace more responsibly our stewardship of the planet. In the distant past, our human ego had viewed animals as *what we experience, they don't experience, they are non-sensing*. We've thought of ourselves to be superior to animals in intelligence. This is the human ego as described by *psychoanalytic theory*, that portion of the human personality which is experienced as the "self" or "I" and is in contact with the external world through the perception of "me". This is changing. Our human experience in regard to the Earth and its inhabitants is transforming to the perception of "we".

What we are learning through veterinary science, zoology, and ethology (the study of sentience in animals) is just how much commonality we share with our fellow beings, such as love and parenting, empathy and grieving, social family structure and biological illness.

"To plumb the depths of animal thinking and feeling," Barbara J. King writes in *How Animals Grieve*, "means to re-assess how we, collectively as a society and individually as persons, treat other animals." Barbara J. King is emeritus professor of anthropology at The College of William and Mary and a freelance science writer with a focus on animals.

In his book *What a Fish Knows: The Inner Lives of Our Underwater Cousins*, my friend and colleague, Jonathan Balcombe, ethologist, author, and speaker, upends our human assumptions about fishes, portraying them as sentient, aware, and social–in other words, much like us. His writing draws on the latest science findings, showing that fishes develop lifelong

What Dogs Hear

bonds with shoal mates, hunt cooperatively, use tools, curry favor, deceive one another, and punish wrongdoers.

The quest for discovery about animal hearing and sound has been the lifelong focus of researchers Henry E. Heffner and Rickye S. Heffner. Their research has had a profound impact on my own understanding and discovery.

Here's their definition of the importance of discovering the connection between sound and animal hearing in their natural environment:

"There have been three main sources of selective pressure on the ability of animals to perceive sound. The first has been the need to detect sound, an ability that enables an animal to determine the presence of sound-producing objects in its environment, which, in most cases, are other animals. The second has been the need to localize the source of a sound so that an animal can either approach or avoid a sound source. Finally, an animal must be able to identify the biological meaning or relevance of the sound so that it may respond appropriately to the sound source. Over the last decade, our knowledge of auditory abilities of animals in general has been the object of study because it was necessary to determine the hearing abilities of large mammals in order to answer certain questions concerning the evolution of animal hearing."

If you will indulge me on a related tangent here, there is a wonderful and poignant story about the discovery of the hidden language of elephant communication. The story shows how scientific breakthroughs unfold when we set aside our human perspective to reveal what is the true life of animals.

I had the privilege of meeting and talking with Katharine Boynton "Katy" Payne, an American zoologist and researcher in the Bioacoustics Research Program at the Laboratory of Ornithology at Cornell University. Dr. Payne studied music and biology in college and, after a decade doing research in the Savanna elephant country in Kenya, Zimbabwe, and Namibia, she founded Cornell's Elephant Listening Project in 1999.

Her discoveries began in 1982 when Dr. Payne and her team observed elephant families and recorded their sounds of communication. The recordings at that time were done using reel-to-reel tape. At first, Dr. Payne discovered subtle vibrations coming from the elephants she was studying. She realized that these vibrations were actually throat sounds, which the elephants were making consciously. It was "a whole new range of communication that no one had studied before in land animals," Payne says.

Payne decoded the sound of a female elephant summoning males during the few days she was in heat, which is audible to humans. In an experiment on the plains of Namibia, Payne played this call on a loudspeaker. Male elephants in the area made a beeline for the speaker.

Then, in 1984, when Dr. Payne and her team returned back to the United States, they played all the collected tapes for review. At one moment, the tape machine developed a technical glitch, which sped up the playback extremely fast. This was a eureka

What Dogs Hear

moment! Where there were long gaps on the tape at normal speed, they could not hear any sounds. At this high speed, they could hear the elephants communicating in multiple tones. The sped-up tape brought the elephant tones into human hearing range, which demonstrated major evidence of their hidden language of communication. The discovery determined that elephants communicate with each other in infrasonic tones below human hearing. This significant discovery on behalf of animal science established a deeper understanding of our animal world. Elephants communicate with each other in frequencies at **14 Hz** and lower. The lesson here is that the importance of setting aside human reference is essential for discovery to uncover truths about animal life.

Speaking with Dr. Payne about her research and acknowledgment of her outstanding discovery has had a tremendous influence on my deep sense and passion for my own research on canine hearing and behavior. I, too, had to set aside my own perspective to gain clearer insights into one of the most overlooked triggers of behavior in dogs: their hearing and the complexity of behaviors in regard to this acute sense. We are discovering that many other species, in comparison to humans, have broader hearing ranges. We must always think outside the box!

CHAPTER 5:

The Psychology of Hearing

Now that we've established the science of sound, variable ear shapes, and important discoveries of animal life, let's move into how your dog perceives their world of sound and what behaviors get triggered by different sounds.

Humans and dogs experience sound differently. There is a branch of science which is the scientific study of sound perception and audiology. This field is called *psychoacoustics* and it describes how humans perceive various sounds. More specifically, it is the branch of science studying the psychological responses associated with sound, including noise, speech, and music.

Dogs also have psychophysical responses associated with sounds just like humans. However, sound is experienced differently by your dog and is, therefore, juxtaposed with our human perception of sound. The term used for this difference is called *psychoacoustic juxtaposition.*

Humans and dogs can perceive the same sound in a much different way. For example, imagine that you're on a city street and you hear a loud siren from a fire truck which startles you. Your spatial-conceptual hearing (where and how far the sound is coming from) triggers your brain to acknowledge, "*This is loud, and this will not harm me.*" Humans can use rational thinking to calm stress responses.

Now, imagine your dog hears the same loud siren and is physically startled. There is no conceptual cognitive pause, just a physical response of needing to get far away from the intensity of the sound and to find a safe space. Feeling the pressure of intense sound in the inner ear, along with low vibrations felt in their body, are the triggers for this behavior. We also know that

What Dogs Hear

some dogs have selective hearing due to conditioning. If your dog lives in a city and sirens are commonly experienced on the street, over time there may not be a dramatic obvious response.

There are other extreme reactions that dogs have, termed *fidget* and *freeze* reactions. During a *fidget* response, the dog seems unsure how to react and may show lip-licking, paw-lifting, pacing, trembling, and other signs of fear. During the *freeze* reaction, the dog remains motionless during the stressful situation. Commonly, you'll see your dog's paw lift up and bend to evaluate the sound or energy.

As pet parents, this special relationship with our dogs in experiencing sound differently is like a *sensory codependency*. We share other sensory experiences more easily with our dogs, such as touch, sight, and taste. However, the canine sense of smell far exceeds ours. "They have up to 300 million olfactory receptors in their noses, versus about six million for us. And the part of their brain dedicated to interpreting these is about forty times larger than ours," says Dr. Michael T. Nappier, DVM, DABVP, of the Virginia Maryland College of Veterinary Medicine. In regard to hearing codependency, we often rely on our dogs to alert us to our surroundings and, in return, our dogs look to us to communicate whether a high alert event is a threat or not.

H.D. Ratnayake, Deputy Director of Sri Lanka's Wildlife Department states, "Animals can be an alert system for us because their senses are not impeded by analytical thinking." Research on both acoustic and seismic communication indicates that elephants can easily pick up vibrations generated from massive earthquakes or tsunamis.

Classical Conditioning

One of the first significant studies of adult canine responses to sound was observed by Ivan Petrovich Pavlov (1849-1936). Pavlov was a Russian physiologist, primarily known for his work in classical conditioning, who called the dogs' anticipatory salivation a *psychic secretion*. Pavlov made informal observations to an experimental test, presenting a stimulus (e.g., the sound of a metronome), then giving the dog food. A metronome is a device used by musicians to mark time at a selected rate by giving a regular ticking sound. Other tools used were bells and tuning forks.

After a few repetitions of using the metronome, the dog started to salivate in response to the stimulus. The idea is that dogs don't *learn* to salivate whenever they see food. This reflex is "hard-wired" into the dog, as I'm sure you regularly see when you open the treat cabinet. In behaviorist terms, food is an unconditioned stimulus and salivation is an unconditioned response. (i.e., a stimulus-response connection that required no learning). Pavlov and his studies of classical conditioning have become famous since his early work between 1890-1930. Classical conditioning is "classical" in that it is the first systematic study of basic laws of learning/conditioning.

I've had my own experience observing classical conditioning behavior in my own dog. One day, my six-year-old dog, *Rags*, (a Lhasa Apso-Wheaten mix) and I were home when the batteries in the smoke detector started to emit a very high pitch, alerting the need for a battery change. The pitch was agitating to my ear and body and absolutely terrifying to Rags. He ran to a room upstairs to get as far away as he could from the sound. Rags remained shivering and panting in a corner with his tail tucked in fear. After I changed the battery and all was well, I then spent time with Rags, talking softly, touching and stroking his body and soothing him back into a sense of feeling safe. In behaviorist terms, back to his *baseline*—his normal balance of behavior.

A few months later, Rags and I were in our backyard enjoying a toy toss, when a red-winged blackbird perched on a bush nearby, chirping. I could hear that the pitch of the chirp was the exact pitch of the smoke detector. I looked at Rags, who'd immediately gone into acute stress from the aural memory of the smoke detector battery pitch. Rags and I went inside, and I again spent time calming him with talk and touch until he returned to his normal heart rate and behavior.

Pavlov's classical conditioning was unfolding before my eyes with Rags' sound trigger as the *pitch* being the theme of his conditioned response, as opposed to the original trigger of the smoke detector or the bird causing his response.

The Importance of the Limbic System

To know your dog is to know your dog's limbic system. This is the area of the brain that regulates emotions. The cerebral cortex is divided up into two areas: the left and right cerebral hemispheres. Within this area is the limbic system, which is a set of structures in the brain that store emotions and memories. It regulates autonomic or endocrine function in response to emotional stimuli and is also involved in reinforcing behavior. It has an essential role in their learning process, just like ours. If you compare a human brain to a dog brain with an MRI, it would show all the same structures, though the dog's brain is smaller.

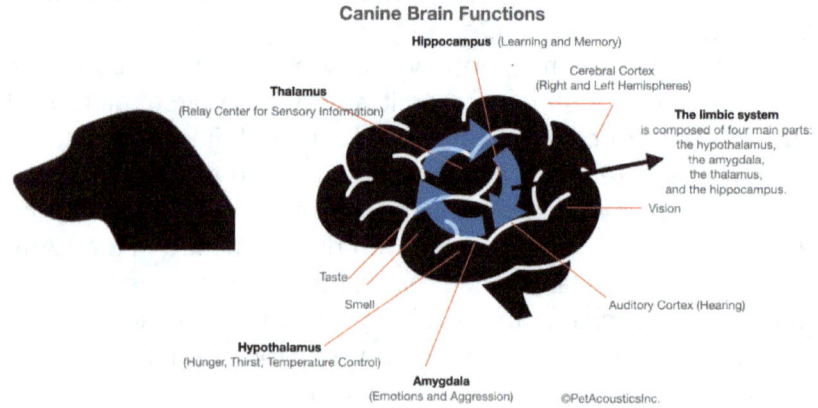

The next story describes the activation of the hippocampus, the area of the brain that holds memory. This activation became apparent with my English Springer Spaniel, Rigby. I live in a country area where we have varying wildlife sightings. One summer, a family of black bears traversed our backyard woods. Rigby learned the word *BEAR* because we loudly exclaimed the word in our own human high-alert behavior when we saw the bears up close through our window. Another day, I commented with enthusiasm to my husband "Wow! What a delicious PEAR!" Rigby's keen ear heard the word, BEAR, which triggered hypervigilance. He then ran to the back door, barking loudly in his protective mode. To his ears, *pear* was *bear* and that's all he needed to hear to activate his memory. Our dogs *are* listening to us!

Two studies, one published in the journal, *Current Biology,* and the other in *Science*, conclude that dogs are listening to everything we're saying. Your dog might not understand *everything* you say, but he listens and pays attention in similar way that humans do. The researchers discovered that dogs—like humans—respond not only to the words we say to them, but also to the emotional tones of our voice.

One of the study's researchers, David Reby, Ph.D., a biologist of Behavior at the Université Jean Monnet, noted, "This is particularly interesting because our results suggest that the processing of speech components in the dog's brain is divided between the two hemispheres in a way that is actually very similar to the way it is separated in the human brain."

Fight-or-Flight

Living in partnership with a dog or a cat, one can witness moments of flight as simple as a response to the sound of a plastic cup dropping on a kitchen floor. The origins of the terms *fight-or-flight* were first defined by Walter Bradford Cannon (1871-1945), a twentieth century American physiologist. His theory states that animals react to threats with a general discharge of the sympathetic nervous system, preparing the animal for fighting or fleeing. The hormones estrogen, testosterone, and cortisol, as well as the neurotransmitters dopamine and serotonin, also reflect how organisms react to stress in animals.

These responses are recognized as the first stage of the general *adaptation syndrome* which regulates stress responses among vertebrates and other organisms. The phrase *fight-or-flight* has been part of our culture in the way that we describe canine stress behaviors. I'd like to take the liberty to add a third word—*balance*—to this description. Why? Because the daily survival of animal life includes seeking a balanced state within their environment. The term *allostasis* describes the ability of an animal to adapt to an environmental change by regulating its physiological state. The concept of allostasis was proposed by the neurophysiologists, Peter Sterling and Joseph Eyer in 1988 as being essential in order to maintain internal viability amid changing conditions. In the wild and in our homes, animals seek balanced states of being through a combination of activity, rest, and play. Lions, as an example, are crepuscular hunters, but spend their day seeking a balance state (allostasis) by resting sixteen to twenty hours of the day. It's not always about fight or flight.

As crepuscular hunters, our domesticated canines look forward to an early breakfast from our kitchens and a dog walk, with various rest times up to ten to fourteen hours a day. Seeking rest is also a response to stress. Muscles relax, energies reboot, and the pleasure of finding the sunny square on the floor to bathe in makes for a healthier and less stressed dog. That's good self-regulating.

Providing your dog with his or her own comfort zone, like a pet bed or a special blanket on a couch with calming music playing, is as essential to their health and wellbeing as providing nutritious food, exercise, and love. Sensory balance with minimal fight-or-flight stress will lead to a longer lifespan for your canine.

For all dogs in our care, helping them adapt to their environment on a physiological level is part of our pet parent responsibility. For example, Rigby, who you now know is my companion and beloved family member, was enjoying his morning rest on the couch next to me while I typed on my laptop. The windows were open and a low rumbling helicopter was passing over my home. From his deep rest, he perked up preparing to flee. He was also evaluating my response, which, if I had shown an abrupt reaction, would have reinforced his triggered behavior. I reached over to his body, laid my hand on his side to share calmness, and said repeatedly, "It's okay," until he laid his head back down into his resting state, releasing a deep exhale. This is a real-time description of how our dogs experience an agitating sound that is outside the home but stimulates a level of canine stress inside the home with muscle tension and high alert flee anticipation.

Whether in a house or in an apartment, our dog's sonic world is very different than ours. We become accepting of the noise and din of appliances, TV, radio, human talk, truck rumbles, planes, sirens... the background sounds of home life. In our dog's life, paws on the floor feel vibrations, from furnaces or air-conditioners, doors opening and closing and bass-enhanced music speakers. If you haven't done this before, get on your hands and knees on the floor and crawl around to feel and hear your home from their perspective. You'll be amazed how different the experience is to their ear height of one to three feet, as opposed to your ear height of five to six feet.

By the way, when I close my laptop from writing this book, Rigby comes right up to me, staring into my face, as if to say, "May I have your attention now?" If I open my laptop, Rigby usually sits

What Dogs Hear

down patiently waiting for me. Just that little puff of air sound that happens when I close my laptop triggers a behavioral change. Thank you, Rigby, for demonstrating classical conditioning.

CHAPTER 6:

Hearing Health—Puppy to Senior

Adopting a puppy into your home is an undeniable joy. Seeing a puppy's playfulness and energy is endearing and entertaining. The first two years of a puppy's life are full of new experiences about their world, and hearing is essential for their learning and training. When a senior dog enters the last few stages of her life, the deep love and bond that has been shared throughout her life in partnership with you is heartwarming. From puppy to senior, it's important to know about each stage of canine hearing health.

Newborn puppies are deaf until about three weeks of age. Until then, a puppy uses her sense of smell to navigate to Mom, siblings, and her surroundings. Eyes begin to open in the second week of life, between ten to fourteen days. Puppies' ears begin to open generally around fourteen to eighteen days old and continue to develop until eight weeks old. Once they have their full hearing ability, they hear twice the frequency levels of humans and sounds four times farther away. When you first bring home a puppy, at this early age, the distinctive sound of your voice becomes imprinted as their new family.

Senior to geriatric dogs, who fall in the age range of seven to fourteen years or older, experience hearing loss as they age. The physical cause is due to degenerative changes in the nerves inside the ear. Loss of hearing is very gradual, so, as a pet parent, you may not notice the change right away. The common form of deafness in dogs is age-related hearing loss, referred to as ARHL. Most dogs experience some degree of ARHL, beginning in the third trimester of life. ARHL begins by affecting the middle- to high- frequency range of sounds, but eventually encompasses the entire range of frequency hearing ability by the geriatric stage.

What Dogs Hear

For seniors, acknowledging their hearing loss is an important step to helping them navigate a new life stage. When dogs have pain or have an illness, they often become stoic, not showing feelings of pain. Fortunately, when they're in our care, we can be on the lookout for signs of hearing loss. Perhaps your dog no longer comes when you whistle, shows changes in daily behaviors, has an increased startle reflex specifically to touch, creates a louder than usual bark to get your attention, increases sleep time or has general apathy. When you have suspicions that there is something wrong with your dog's hearing, take her to the veterinarian for evaluation and possible treatment.

Whether your senior dog can no longer hear or is deaf from birth, you can observe her sense of smell and sight in greater use. They are still their wonderful doggy beings; they'll just require extra attention from their caregiver for safety in their daily life.

Since you won't be using your voice to get her attention, you have to learn other ways of communicating with your senior. A dog will use her eyes to observe activity more closely and watch people's physical movement for cues as to what is happening. For example, your dog will feel the new air flow created by the opening and closing of a door. Your senior will feel the vibrations on the floor from footsteps and will see lights turn on and off. Sight, motion, smell, and changes in energy are senior dogs' new methods of navigating. A smile from your face and reassuring touches will give your dog confidence that everything is okay in this phase of life.

One technique that I have recommended to pet parents with a puppy or a senior dog is to create a scent trail game by dabbing a small amount of lavender essential oil around the house. I recommend lavender because this scent is known to be calming for dogs. Breathing the lavender helps to reduce their anxiety and stress. Make a scent trail for your dog to follow as their nose-work in your home. This also works well with high value treats like cheese or bits of meat. The more smell, the better! This creates a fun activity and will give your dog confidence.

You may know of the invention of the dog whistle, which is used in sports hunting. The dog whistle was developed in 1876 by Francis Galton, who was an anthropologist. The whistle produces sounds that are between 23,000 kHz to 54,000 kHz, inaudible to humans. To our ear it sounds like a hissing sound. If your dog has the ability to hear some high frequency sounds, the whistle can be used to get their attention or signal them to come into the house from the backyard. Only do this at a reasonable distance from your dog and definitely not inside the house. If too close, it may further damage your dog's hearing. There are downloadable dog whistle apps to try. You might want to ask your veterinarian or a behaviorist if your dog would benefit from this.

Hearing and Sleep

Canine ears, like human ears, never close! When we sleep, our ears are still hearing, though our brains go in and out of sound response according to the different stages of sleep. There are two basic types of sleep: REM-sleep (rapid eye movement) and non-REM sleep, over three different stages.

- Stage One occurs right after you fall asleep and is very short.
- Stage Two is a light sleep. Heart rate slows and body temperature drops.
- Stage Three is the deep sleep stage.

Each of these stages is linked to specific brain waves and neuronal activity. It is a fascinating subject to look into, as we do it every day of our lives.

Research has identified that the brain waves of dogs during sleep are comparable to those of humans. Have you seen your dog twitch when she is sleeping? This is when your dog has entered REM sleep or rapid eye movement. Compared to humans who have 25% of REM deep sleep, dogs only need 10% of REM for health. Getting quality sleep every day is a key component of your dog's health at any age.

What Dogs Hear

If your dog experiences agitating noises while home alone, your dog may not be getting sufficient rest. This is important because during sleep, dogs—just like humans—experience allostatic regulation, which is the balancing of cell function. How much sleep a dog needs depends on the breed of the dog, the size of the dog, their diet, daily walks, and amount of play exercise.

Canine rest periods weave in and out of daily life. As sleep or rest is a major part of their day for health and rebalance, the acoustics and sounds in their environment are key factors. If their environment is noisy, like the reverberating cement walls of animal shelters, dogs hardly get a chance to rest deeply. In a veterinary kennel, the same acoustic issues can apply which can exacerbate the emotional stress of separation anxiety. Have you seen your dog go into a deep rest right after a veterinary checkup? Just being home helps your dog succumb to the quiet and safety to release muscle tension due to stress. There's no place like home!

When a puppy is learning to be home alone, they can experience acute separation anxiety. The release of the adrenaline hormone causes a state of stress and if the stress continues, cortisol—known as the stress hormone—is released into the body, causing your dog to be anxious and reactive. During the night, if you've ever tried to sleep while your puppy is being crate-trained, you have heard with your own ears the level of stress they are experiencing. It's understandable that your puppy just wants to be cuddled and be close to you for deep relaxation, but, just like a baby, they need to self-regulate into a state of relaxation at some point.

A major focus of my research has been to help animals self-regulate into states of calm and relaxation by altering their sonic environment. As I wrote in the preface, I invented a process of modifying sounds in music called *species-specific music*. At a certain level of high and low frequencies, alert behaviors are triggered. Eliminating these high and low frequencies in the music design helps an animal release stress and become balanced in their listening environment. For puppy and senior hearing health, playing music with calming sounds aids sleep and promotes well-being.

"I had a new puppy that had separation issues not only when I'd leave the house, but when I'd leave the room. He would cry, bark, and even go to the bathroom in his crate when I'd leave. As soon as I turn on the ©Pet Tunes Speaker and the music starts playing, it totally calms down my pup. It is a great item and is really helping the household. My older dog seems to like it too!"

"As a veterinarian behaviorist, I learned of a wonderful tool to use with my dogs and my patients. Pet Tunes for dogs. My own dog Joe, a senior Dachshund, began to manifest pain in his spine. The diagnosis was from a slipped disc, which could still be handled with medications and absolute rest, otherwise, it would worsen his condition. This meant that my dog could only move for the essentials: to go to the bathroom and settle in his bed. Here, the key was providing environmental enrichment of various kinds. In different contexts, I began to place the music to see that she could be calmer at night, resting well. During the day, when she was alone, I played the music and when I returned, she was resting in a deep sleep. The music was an important part of improving her well-being. Now, she's a healthy dog and we both rest listening to ©Pet Tunes."

CHAPTER 7:

Using Technology to See Sound

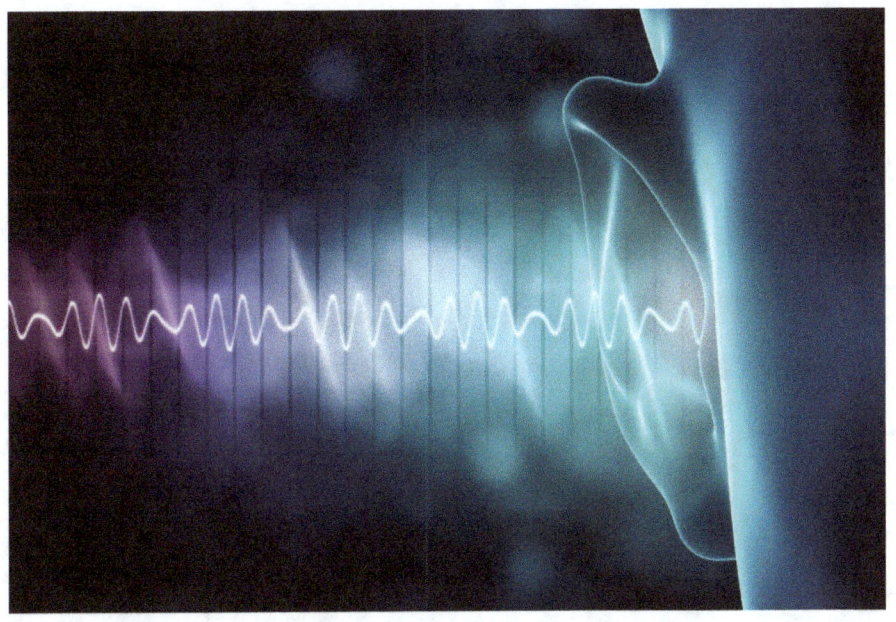

We have defined sound as frequencies, decibels, and environments that affect your dog's behavior. Now, let's utilize technology to see what your dog is experiencing sonically in your home, in your car or anywhere you and your dog go.

Decibel (dB) Reader

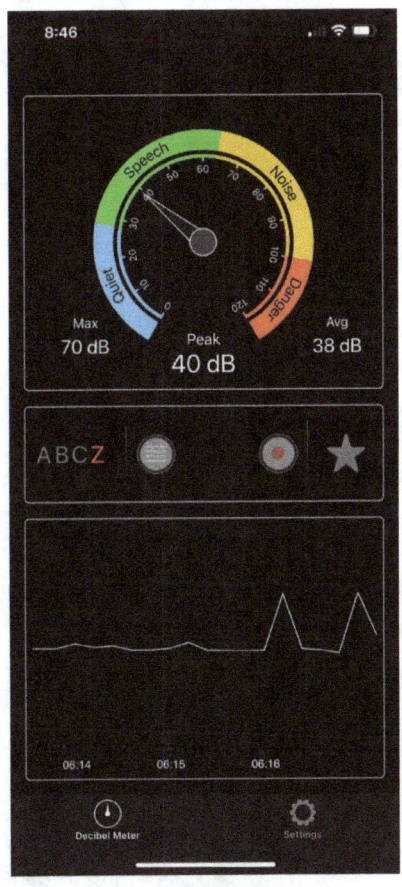

What Dogs Hear

First, let's download a free decibel (dB) reader on the App Store to visually understand the volume of sounds. For a quick choice to start with, I recommend the app, dBMeter. Once you've downloaded the app, you will see the measurement of volume categories from Quiet to Speech to Noise to Danger levels. You can have fun seeing sound levels right away! Try to speak at different volume levels into your smartphone or other device and watch the meters change. This will give you a good sense of the fluctuations of volume in your dog's environment.

We know that dogs have a comfort hearing level from 60 dB to 80 dB. Beyond 80 dB, sounds become an agitation to the canine ear and, therefore, will start to trigger alert behavior. For human reference, the Occupational Safety and Health Administration (OSHA) provides decibel guidelines for hearing health in the workplace but they also apply to daily life.

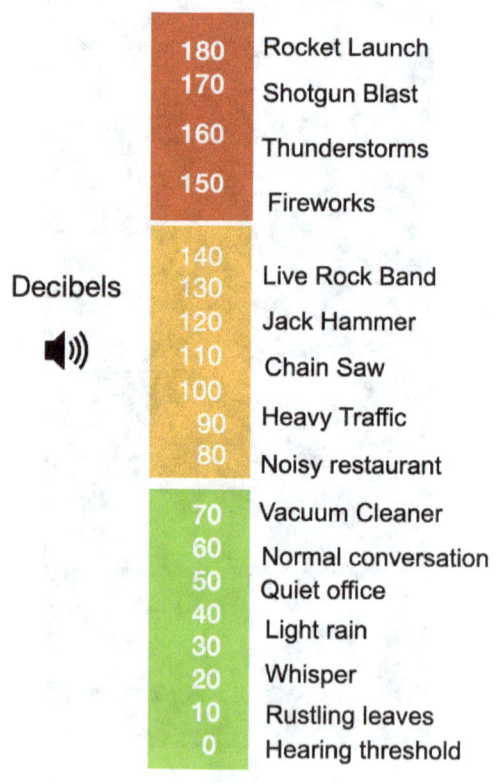

You can easily evaluate the dB levels of your dog's environment by looking for the range from 60 dB to 80 dB, such as normal conversation and household appliances. Above 80 dB your dog will feel the beginnings of stress and alert behavior. If the range falls below 60 dB, that means less volume will not have any negative reactive behaviors.

You can use the meter outdoors to identify the volume level from street traffic, sirens or even wind. It's also a great tool to use for your cat's response to sounds in their environment.

Frequency (Hz) Reader

Now, let's download a frequency (Hz) reader from the App Store to visually understand the pitch of sounds. There are several choices of applications but for now, I recommend the app, FFT PLOT. (Or the Simple FFT app which is free.) This will indicate ultrasonic (high) and infrasonic (low) sounds that you can't hear. *Ultrasonic* refers to sound waves with a frequency above the upper limit of human hearing, 20,000 Hz. Dogs can hear ultrasonic sounds above human hearing. *Infrasonic* refers to sound waves with a frequency below the lower limit of human hearing. The app has limits since the average device can only register sounds up to 20,000 Hz. Special equipment is needed to identify sounds above and below human hearing. Additionally, devices can only broadcast a limited amount of sound. But you can still see sound levels beyond your hearing ability to gain insight into your dog's hearing world.

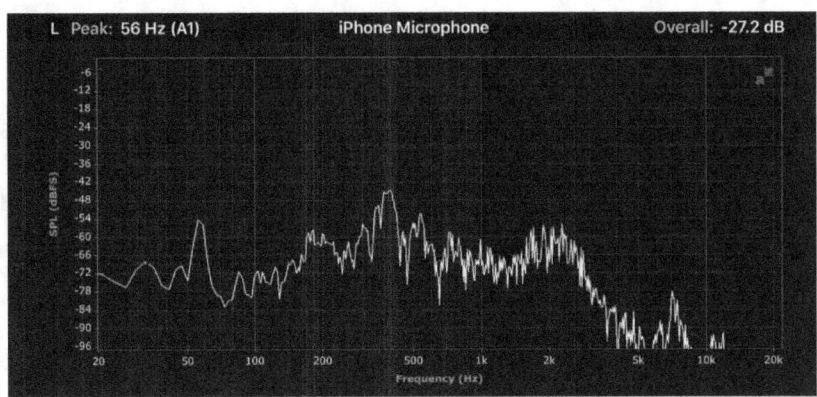

What Dogs Hear

The above chart shows the human hearing range from 20 Hz to 20,000 Hz. There is a peak on this chart at about 400 Hz. It is amazing to see the quick fluctuation of sound in the air once you have your app on and capturing sound. It will give you a clear understanding of why there is constant movement of canine and feline ears throughout the day detecting sound variations.

You will see that the dB readings have a minus sign and the letters SPL, which stand for *sound pressure level*. For sound and noise, we normally compare what is considered to be the quietest sound an ear can hear and add the letters SPL. This means that anything louder than the quietest sound an ear can hear will always have a positive dB SPL. The decibel is used for logarithmic relative measurements from sound pressure level to electrical standards. Each one has its particular reference zero defined to make each scale useful. Remember that 0 dB is not positioned as no signal, because that would be negative infinity. Even 0 dB SPL is actually a sound intensity. Simply put, it's the threshold of human hearing.

In the pet industry, ultrasonic dog collars and other devices have been developed to stop a dog from barking. The reason the dog stops barking is because of the intense pressure in the dog's ear from a high frequency intensity, which startles the dog into a freeze behavior. I will not leave my opinion here as to whether this is a good tool or not as some dogs may need this kind of abrupt behavior device. It's up to every caregiver to decide on best training practices.

Using technologies to evaluate your dog's hearing environment are valuable tools for his ear health. So the next time there is a thunderstorm or firework event, take out your dB and Hz readers and see what your dog is truly experiencing with sound.

CHAPTER 8:

Test Your Dog's Hearing

When your dog goes for a veterinary checkup, the doctor will regularly check your dog's ears to help spot problems, such as ear infections. Your veterinarian will also observe your dog's hearing ability. They'll likely check to see if your dog responds to sounds outside their field of vision and take note if your dog has involuntary flicking or twitching of the ears, called *Pryor's reflex* in response to sound.

You can test your own dog's hearing by standing in a location out of sight from your dog and make a loud sound by clapping your hands, whistling, or banging a spoon on a pot. Have another person stand near your dog and ask that person to look for a head turn or a change in ear position. If there's no head turn or altered ear position, then you would want to get further testing done.

A professional veterinary procedure to test a dog's hearing is called The Brainstem Auditory Evoked Response or BAER hearing test. Dr. Ellis. R. Loew, a physiologist at the veterinary college at Cornell University describes the details of the hearing test.

"There are defects that occur in the pathways between the ear and the brain. If those defects are present, then the animal is deaf. Most of these defects are congenital. However, you can't tell necessarily if they're deaf simply from their behavior when they're just little pups. So, many years ago, a test was developed originally for humans that basically measures the electrical response of the ear. The brain center would be given a stimulus such as a series of clicks. This stimulates the cells in the inner ear. The clicks fire a nerve impulse that travels along a nerve to another group of cells. The sound daisy-chains its way along these nerve impulses and, if everything is fine, you get a series of sound waves that shows on a software program that

What Dogs Hear

correspond with the nerve pathway, showing that it is working. If you find that the animal has some congenital defect, you won't see these waves; you'll get a picture of a flat line. The hearing defect can be one ear or both ears. The test is painless, quick, and the pet parent can be there with their dog."

As this is a book on hearing health, it is important to care for your dog's ears as part of their grooming routine. To avoid ear infections and to maintain health, veterinarians recommend cleaning your dog's ears periodically. Ask your veterinarian or vet tech about the best method to use.

CHAPTER 9:

Classical Music, TV, Radio. What Works?

Classical Music

I am a fifth-generation classical musician and composer in my family, going back approximately 250 years. I've enjoyed a career as a recording artist and composer, and performed in many, many concert halls and festivals. I'm listing my music history here to share with you what I know about classical music as a tool for calming animal behaviors. This also includes two decades of research and clinical studies proving the effects of music on animals. These studies have been published in industry magazines and veterinary science journals.

Pet parents often leave a TV, radio or sound system on while they are away from home. These are good instincts on the part of caregivers who realize that their dogs need the company of sound to make them feel safe in their environment. What are the best devices to guarantee behavioral calm? Is what we use to broadcast sound from as important as what sounds we are playing? Do you need a different type of device to be used in the home, at the kennel or in a shelter? Here are the facts on each of these commonly used tools of TV, radio, and classical music for canine hearing environments to help you provide what is best.

Studies have proven that music *is* an effective calming experience for animals. Music consists of tone, volume, and vibrations—all aspects of their listening world. Playing classical music has emerged as a more effective calming style for dogs as compared to other music genres, such as rock or highly active music.

First, there is an interesting history to the use of classical music for animals in the twentieth century. During World War II, European farmers would bring a radio into their cow barns to

What Dogs Hear

keep up with the latest news events. On the BBC radio in England, there were programs broadcasting soothing arrangements of classical music to keep folks calm during these terrorizing times. I know this fact because my father, Michael Spivakowsky, who was the conductor of the Stradavari Orchestra on BBC Radio during this time, broadcast hours of classical music arrangements in understanding of this purpose. Amazingly, the farmers who brought radios into their barns during the war, unexpectedly discovered that their cows produced more milk listening to classical music programs.

Fast forward sixty years—in 2001, a study by scientists Dr. Adrian North and Liam MacKenzie at the Music Research Group at the University of Leicester School of Psychology UK, played different music of different tempos for herds of Friesian cattle. "Results found that dairy cows produce more milk when listening to REM's 'Everybody Hurts' or Beethoven's 'Pastoral Symphony' than when subjected to Wonderstuff's 'Size of a Cow' or the Beatles' 'Back In The USSR'. Their milk yield rose by 0.73 litres per cow per day when they were exposed to slow music rather than fast music." North and MacKenzie postulated that "Calming music can improve milk yield, probably because it reduces stress."

There are, however, misconceptions about classical music as a choice to calm canine behavior. Classical music may appear to be less active and, therefore, soothing to the listener, but remember the term *psychoacoustics juxtaposition*? What we experience sonically is not what our dogs experience sonically. Not all classical music guarantees calm for a dog's behavior because, in close listening, there is a broad spectrum of dynamics, pitches, and jolts of volume. For example, in recordings of *Beethoven's 9th Symphony*, which I have played as a violinist in orchestras, there are unexpected increases in volume from the tympani section to loud entrances from the brass section, and fluctuations of loud and soft phrases occurring throughout the work which concludes with a chorus of a hundred human voices. This is what makes classical music emotional and exciting for the human listener. By the way, the term *classical* means music written in the European tradition during a period lasting approximately from

1750 to 1830, when forms such as the symphony, concerto, and sonata were standardized. In some people's opinion, classical music is a bit boring and, therefore, should be calming for dogs. Subjective music opinions are fine, but please don't say this to a Beethoven or Brahms's music lover! If you are going to play classical music for your dog, use your decibel and frequency readers to observe the music changes from your playing device and then see what works best for your dog's sense of calm.

TV

Flat panel TVs have tiny speakers that are either pointed downward or facing the wall in back. Though the sound may be reflecting off the wall, the small surface area results in a weak projected sound. Minimal disbursement of sound doesn't necessarily engage a dog's ears, especially if the TV is three feet above a dog's head. "They orient to things they're interested in, look at it for a couple of minutes and go 'hmm, interesting,' and then look away," said Nicholas Dodman, renowned veterinary behaviorist.

Does your dog watch TV? In 2013, a study published in the journal, *Animal Cognition* showed that dogs could identify images of other dogs among pictures of humans and other animals, using their visual sense alone. Depending on the breed, some dogs are visually stimulated from the colors and movement on the TV which can be very stimulating but not ideal if the goal is to calm your dog from any stress while home alone.

Did you know TV commercials are purposely louder in between programs to grab our human hearing attention? Over the past few years, advertisers have been embedding subliminal ultrasonic tones into commercials which humans *can't* hear but dogs can. Also, high frequencies that we *can* hear are inserted to get our attention, but can also be very agitating to our dogs while we are expecting them to remain calm while home alone.

You can test TV commercial levels using your decibel reader. You'll be amazed at how much louder the advertisements are as

What Dogs Hear

compared to the regular programming. Before you choose TV as company for your dog, consider these sonic variables along with programming choices for your dog's behavior while home alone.

Radio

Radios are often placed four to six feet off the ground on a shelf or on a kitchen counter. The sound emitted from radio travels a short distance in the air at an average listening volume. The sensitivity output or the sound pressure level (SPL) of a speaker gives a rating of how loud the speaker will play with a specific amount of power at a specific distance. Since radio emits sound at a short distance, increasing the volume is the only way to fill a room with sound. That would be near the threshold of comfort in canine hearing which is within the 60 dB - 80 dB of range. Whether broadcasting music or talk radio with commercials, remember what we experience as reasonable is not necessarily what your dog would find comforting or effective for behavioral calm.

As a caregiver, listen to the sounds that you want to leave on for your dog and evaluate if it has a positive, negative, or non-effect on behavior.

CHAPTER 10:

Thunderstorms and Fireworks

The intensity of sounds from thunderstorms is one of the most common causes of canine acute stress behaviors. Crashes of thunder and lightning strikes that we can hear have an agitating effect on us as well. The shift in barometric pressure is an initial indicator that a storm is approaching, and it is felt by humans as well as animals. When a storm is occurring in your area, it is heartbreaking to see your wonderful dog panting, pacing, and drooling in a highly anxious state. You'd like to hold your dog and help her break out of this behavior, but, more often than not, your loving efforts are to no avail. Dogs and cats can also suffer static shocks in the buildup to a thunderstorm. If you become nervous or anxious yourself, your dog may mirror your behavior. "There's something about their makeup that makes their thresholds for developing this, or their ability to recover, lower than that of other animals," says Lore Haug, DVM, a veterinary behaviorist at Texas Veterinary Behavior Services.

The decibel range of a thunderstorm is between 100 dB to 115 dB, way beyond the safety range for canine ears. Thunder also occurs in the infrasonic range (below 20 Hz), which is inaudible to humans. During a storm, pressure will occur in a dog's ear, which is experienced as a pulsating sensation. Both ultrasonic and infrasonic sounds can be observed in the same thunderstorm. A clap of thunder can reach 120 dB, so, you can understand why a thunderstorm is an intense experience for their ears and ours.

A dog will want to escape to safety, and the shift to flight-or-fight behavior can happen quickly. Pet parents have shared with me stories of their dog jumping into a bathtub, shaking under a bed, and running right through electric fences. If a dog lives in an area that has rolling thunderstorms due to afternoon heat, the dog will develop storm phobia, which will need a behaviorist and calming tools to overcome. There are also hereditary predispositions to fear or anxiety reactive to thunderstorms, especially common in some hunting and herding breeds which includes the German Shepherd, Australian Shepherd, Labrador Retriever, Border Collie, Havanese, Shorthaired Pointer, Vizsla, and Bichon Frise.

Young dogs and senior dogs display fear of thunderstorm sounds for different reasons than adult dogs. To a young dog, storms are a new experience to learn and they can be terrifying as awareness grows. Senior and geriatric dogs, whose hearing has greatly diminished, will still experience the pressure of sound by absorbing vibrations in their bodies and through their paws, which can be disorienting.

"That fear response becomes classically conditioned," says veterinary behaviorist Lisa Radosta, who practices at Florida Veterinary Behavior Service in West Palm Beach. "Maybe the first storm isn't traumatic, but, over time, the fear response becomes triggered by elements of the storm."

To assist a young pup in desensitizing to loud noises like thunderstorms or fireworks, you can pop bubble wrap in a room where they are. First, use your dB App to test the loudness of the *pop!* yourself. Have your dog smell the sheet of bubble wrap to know where the sound is coming from. Then, keeping a distance from your dog in the room, pop one bubble, then stop and say, "It's okay." During another session, pop two bubbles, then repeat saying, "It's okay." Evaluate your pup's response to see if it lessens reactive behavior as you increase the experience. Make sure to keep the bubble wrap away from your dog's head and ears. Your reassurance by saying, "It's okay" will be good practice for when you and your dog are on the street and there's a loud pop sound that may startle your dog. Desensitizing your dog to street sounds, trucks, and car horns is a good practice when they are young to minimize noise phobias later on.

For adult dogs, playing calming canine music will mask the thunderstorm sounds. For senior and geriatric dogs, it's best to confine their movement to one area or room to prevent injury during agitated roaming.

Fireworks- the big horrible bang for a dog

In years past, people would gather at a large park or river shore area to enjoy a celebration with fireworks. The event would generally be coordinated by a city, town or organization and there would be a safe distance between the fireworks and the crowd of people. Now, with the availability of fireworks sold in stores for the consumer, fireworks can be heard at any time of year and as close as your neighbor's backyard. That is fun and convenient but really bad news for dogs and cats!

Every July 4th, there are inevitably reports of dogs missing from their homes due to firework events. It is difficult to stop the flight response when there are intense sound waves close by. Due to this, dogs have run through screen doors, destroyed furniture, and fled the home for days until found.

If you are watching fireworks that are about a kilometer (1000 meters) away, the light takes only three millionths of a second to reach you. The sound takes about three seconds. Sound waves are much slower because they require a medium (mass of molecules) to travel. Fireworks produce a sound output that is in the 150 dB to 175 dB range. Fireworks generate a higher noise level than firecrackers or gunshots.

"There are three types of noises from every firework: a screeching, a whistle, and a bang. Fireworks are filled with lead oxide, which turns into lead atoms as the firework explodes and heats up. Half of the narrow tube remains empty and once the firework is lit up, the empty part of the tube will vibrate and make the whistling sound," as explained by the American Chemical Society.

"In addition, firecrackers are poisonous and their explosion releases harmful particles, such as fine dust (PM10), that is toxic to inhale. Therefore, fireworks represent a danger both to animals and humans who live in areas where they explode, or in relatively distant locations when the wind transports the particles. There is also a risk of ingestion of the residue of fireworks and firecrackers. The proximity animals are to the areas where the firecrackers are made often causes burns and damage to the eyes."

What Dogs Hear

As I am writing this book with a chapter about fireworks, I paid close attention this year to the local July 4th event near my home. I was shocked to discover how much my entire home vibrated from each firework explosion. I placed my hand on the walls and windows in the room where Rigby was and felt every intense vibration. Rigby was tense, but he was also wearing an Ultra Calmer collar which I designed for him to ease his and other dogs' for sound stress. I'd like to share how I came to invent this device.

My passion for innovating effective tools for pet parents to resolve thunderstorm and firework stress culminated in 2016. I have talked about my beloved dog Rigby, who was my inspiration to create a solution. When Rigby was a year and half, he showed his first signs of stress due to an intense thunderstorm. It was hard to observe him pacing and being highly agitated. No amount of soft talk or touch could break his state of acute stress. That moment inspired me to invent the Ultra Calmer collar device. I spent many months thinking what would be the best device for a dog to overcome sound stress during storms and fireworks. I definitely wanted it to be easily snapped on by a caregiver and for the dog to be able to pace or hide while wearing it. I created frequency-based music of which the Hz levels were modified for canine ears, already clinically proven to calm dogs. I developed a patent for the Ultra Calmer music device which came in three different collar sizes for small, medium and large dogs. Then, I developed a SafeVolume® Mode so that the volume level was comfortable to maintain a consistent hearing response. The product made its debut in 2016 and has helped many dogs, including my precious Rigby, ride out a thunderstorm or endure local fireworks with behavioral calm and minimal stress.

Here are two pet parent's comments.

> "I bought the Ultra Calmer last fall for my golden mix, who is afraid of thunder. Yesterday, as the storms rolled through, I put it on him. There was no heavy panting, no nervous following me around. He laid down and appeared to be fine. I didn't have to give him any tranquilizers. Thank you!!!"

"Lex is terrified of fireworks. At the first boom I placed the collar with preloaded music on him and he fell asleep on the couch. Normally he's hiding in the bathroom."

Gunfire

Almost all firearms create noise that is from 140 dB to 174 dB levels. A small. 22-caliber rifle can produce noise around 140 dB. Some dogs can be desensitized to gunshot levels, as they are needed to be alongside police, military, and for search-and-rescue missions. The training for gun dogs and hunting dogs starts at puppy age. Not all dogs in this training are going to be physiologically capable for this job. For many dogs, sounds of this intensity are traumatizing. The following story of one dog's experience is a true depiction of how gunfire can affect their hearing.

The Story of Shai

Dogs can suffer irreversible hearing loss caused by the proximity to the intense sound of gunfire. With this in mind, I'd like to share a story of a dog named Shai. Shai, a Golden Retriever, was a service dog to his person, Patty. His job was to provide Patty stability for walking in public places. He was a great companion to her. One day, Patty and Shai were invited to an event in her town to honor the fallen, as her husband was and still is the Chief of Police. Shai and Patty were seated in a section near the stage. Unexpectedly, close to where they were seated, a twenty-one-gun salute was fired by the honor guard. This was a shock to Patty as it had been added to the event without her knowledge. After that trauma, Patty saw noise phobia develop gradually in Shai. First, he showed being noise sensitive to popping sounds. "The public is full of popping sounds," Patty observed. "Then, the 4th of July brought a week of fireworks next door in our neighborhood. Then, after that, there was an incident at a restaurant where he was sleeping under the booth when the staff suddenly started popping paper bags right next to our table for a birthday. It woke him to the sound memory of gunshots again. Shai's noise sensitivity became more extreme. Then, after that, we were at church when the minister started doing loud single repeated claps into the microphone. Again, Shai was sound asleep. It sounded like gunshots and startled him again. We couldn't get him out and away from it." After this sequence of events, Shai showed resistance and fear going into public places where he heard popping sounds as related to the gunfire trauma. Patty realized the sound sensitivity was much worse, so she and her husband made the decision to put him on leave from working in public until they could find a veterinary behaviorist to help Shai. They brought Shai to the Mississippi State University College of Veterinary Medicine - Animal Health Center. It was determined that Shai suffered from gunshot and fireworks phobia, storm phobia, and separation anxiety, all caused by the twenty-one-gun salute trauma. "He has canine PTSD, but they don't have a behavior code yet for this. But he has what some war dogs get," Dr. Calder, the veterinarian behaviorist, commented. It was recommended to retire Shai from being a service dog. "I told her that retiring him would mean retiring me from public," Patty responded. Dr. Calder agreed to treat him but only gave a 50/50 chance of recovering and getting back to work in public. Shai was given medications and placed through a behavior modification program.

I know of Patty and Shai's story because a trainer recommended the *Ultra Calmer* collar for Shai. Shai started wearing the collar in public places, along with other calming tools. Patty describes how the collar worked. "Shai progressed so well on his behavior modification training that he was weaned off his medication. He returned full-time to working in public without meds. He wore only his collar. He no longer needed his medication during storms—just the collar. Shai's veterinary behaviorist was so surprised and pleased with his recovery that she used him to do a case presentation to her peers." A happy ending for Patty and Shai that I was truly grateful to be part of.

CHAPTER 11:

The Pitch of Your Voice

You and your partner have decided to adopt a dog from your local shelter. You found a wonderful, tail-wagging, mixed-breed dog that you both fell in love with. Papers were signed, the dog was driven home, and the adjustment began for you both and your new family member. After a few days, you were communicating with your dog in an endearing high-pitched tone and his behavior was adjusting nicely. But as soon as your partner came home and said, "Fido, I'm home" in a deep low voice, your dog cowered with tail-tucked and ears down low in response. This was a surprise. You were both doing your best to make your dog feel safe and comfortable, but something was not right. What was your dog telling you?

Fido responded well to the high vocal pitch of one person while the other person's voice, with its low, vocalized tones, induced fear and stress. There can be several reasons for this response. It could be that your partner has a different energy that can be perceived as scary if the dog's nurturing and socializing had been cut short before proper development. A low voice can indicate a reprimand or an abusive behavior that could trigger a previous fear. It can be that Fido is relating the low voice pitch to his previous life in a memory that is stored in the hippocampus function of the brain. Simply changing the tone and pitch of the partner's voice to a higher vocal expression can help the dog feel safe over time. This can be a simple solution to a human voice fear trigger.

In February 2014, researcher Dr. Attila Andics at the University of Budapest revealed that a dog's brain reacts to voices in the same way as a human brain. Eleven dogs and owners were each placed in an MRI scanner and played over 200 different sounds, from car sounds and whistles to human sounds and dog noises. The researchers found that a similar region—the temporal pole, which is the most anterior part of the temporal lobe—was activated when both the animals and people heard human voices. "We do know there are voice areas in humans, areas that respond more strongly to human sounds, than any other types of sounds," Dr. Andics explained. "The location (of the activity) in the dog brain is very similar to where we found it in the human brain. The fact that we found these areas exist at all in the dog brain is a surprise—it is the first time we have seen this in a non-primate." The fact that emotionally charged sounds, such as crying or laughter, prompted similar responses in humans as they did with the dogs might explain why dogs are so attuned to human emotions.

Let's look further into the beginnings of canine communication. We know that dogs hear higher frequencies better than we do. Newborn puppies' survival instincts prompt high frequency utterances from the minute they are born to communicate with Mom. A high-pitched whimper says, "I'm lost," alerting Mom's ears to track the little one and reach over to bring the puppy close to her. For survival in the wild, mother dogs don't bark, because that would make the whelps vulnerable to an attack.

In my studies, I've discovered that animals have two types of vocal communications: a public voice and a private voice. As we learned through Dr. Katy Payne's discovery of elephant communication, private family communications were in infrasonic levels, below our human hearing, and their public voice communications are expressed as barks, grunts, trumpets, and cries, which are audible to humans.

Our dogs also have two types of vocal communications. Canine public voice communications are different dynamics of barks, growls, and howls, and can easily be heard by the human ear. However, there is a private voice shared with their pet parent which is intended for family communication. Private voice communications are usually high-frequency utterances. Additionally, dogs express soft volume breathy utterances that come from their chest, throat, and nose. These sound like a whistle with air pressure coming from the snout. Sometimes, it is a combination of high pitches on top of breathy utterances. These sounds are at a very subtle volume as they are meant to be just for you. If you are sitting and your dog needs something, she will stand right in front of you, voicing high pitched whines, waiting to be acknowledged. Acknowledging her vocal communication requires *your* hearing ability and attention to her communication. I believe our listening attention to their public and private communications is an important interpretation skill to help us be aware of our dog's needs.

As a sound behaviorist, I have learned that dogs use a wide range of pitches to communicate. In turn, dogs respond to our pitches of communication which also requires a variety of frequencies. Sometimes, our normal conversational tones may not be enough to get a desired result when we're training our dog. Recently, I had a friend ask me to help her with a two-year-old Jack Russell she was having some difficulty training. I spent some time observing how she was talking with her dog. She was saying all the right commands, but she spoke in a very, very soft voice. Yes, dogs have great hearing, but they will exercise selective hearing if they don't feel the energy and intention of the request. Just by helping my friend speak louder and more assertively while training, I was able to help her get cooperation from her dog.

Another communication technique is the "clicker" sound. This can be done with the side of the mouth and tongue, releasing the tongue tight from the side of the cheek to make a *click* sound. The intensity of the click is a great attention getter for dogs as is widely known by the use of the clicker training tool. When Rigby and I are out for our walk and I need to change our direction, I use a few mouth clicks and say, "This way," in a high pitch. With traffic sounds and vibrations, my directives need to be dynamic enough to access his three-foot hearing level along with my leash directions. If there is a foreign item on the street that I don't want Rigby to nose or eat, I will give the training command, "Leave it!" making sure that I voice this in a low dynamic tone to make clear the immediacy of my ask. As dogs are acutely aware of their sonic environment, their response to your pitch of voice is a natural way to keep your agreement going smoothly.

What Dogs Hear

Each of these four levels of communication requires a different dynamic of the human voice.

- **Affection** (soft, high pitch) - play, cuddle, touch, talking, calming, empathy
- **Conversational** (normal voice pitch) - natural speaking tones, talking
- **Command** (directive, lower pitch) - behavioral training, leash communication, play guidance, agility training, service dog training
- **Reprimand** (forceful, low pitch) - curtailing excessive behavior, avoidance of danger

You can use your Frequency app to see the difference in range of your voice when you speak in an affectionate tone, in a commanding tone, or in a reprimanding tone. The range will show the exact changes in frequencies and volume levels of your voice.

Amazingly, a dog can learn, on average, up to 165 words. Adding intentional dynamics and pitches to your vocabulary will refine your communication. You can do this experiment for yourself to understand the difference between the tone of speaking the word and the word itself. Try speaking a reprimanding phrase, such as, "Put that shoe down", in a high affectionate soft voice and your dog may wag her tail and not interpret this as, "I've done something wrong," but feel the gentleness of your voice and may expect a treat even though you're expressing strong meaning words. Matching your intention with the word will be the best way to communicate to your dog.

If you listen closely to a dog's range of vocalizations, you will hear a vast range of dynamics coming from their snout. Dogs communicate their language from vocalizing in two different ways: with an open snout or a closed snout. The snout entails the nose, mouth, and the jaw. Communications are also expressed from the chest, throat, and nose.

Open-snout vocalizations:
- Panting
- Short, breathy sounds
- Barks
- Howls
- Growls

Closed-snout vocalizations:
- Whimpers
- Whines
- Whistles
- High-frequency utterances
- Low chest utterances
- Soft breath with harmonics

A *harmonic* is a sound wave that has a frequency that is an integer multiple above a fundamental tone. This means that when you hear a tone, the fundamental, there are tones that exist in a specific series of intervals called harmonics. Most of these tones are above human hearing but exist in the air. If you listen very, very, carefully, you can hear some of these harmonics accompanied with breath coming from your dog's snout.

A dog's language communication has a vast range of sounds, which is beyond the bark that most people identify as a dog talking. A dog's entire voice range can traverse four octaves, or approximately forty-eight notes. A dog's bark—their public voice—is easy to acknowledge, but if you spend time listening more , you may hear her high-frequency voice when it's time for dinner. When she is at rest, you can hear deep exhales with moans of contentment emanating from her chest. When she is in a dream state, she utters high frequency sounds when she is on that imaginary chase. As she stands up from a resting position, there are rhythmic, breathy sounds. When she wants something from you, she whimpers in a high pitch. When she shows aggression to another dog on the street nearby, she will have different barks according to how she evaluates the other dog as friend or foe. If she senses a friendly dog, she may produce a howling call. If she senses an aggressive dog, she will bark deeply from her chest. Just like a trained singer, dogs move air from their chest through their throat to their mouth to express themselves. Each part of their upper body uses pressure to move air to create communication with their world for response and interaction.

A dog's bark can explode as an intense first sound and end into a sequence of panting. Some barks are short and consist of one pitch. Others have a rhythm with an equal interval of time between each bark. There are barks that start off high in pitch and then go down to the chest before returning to the high pitch. There are combinations of barks that have longer phrases, especially when your dog is excited, with breathy panting starting the sequence.

If you are indifferent to your dog's bark, she will continue to escalate the pitch until you acknowledge the communication in some way. Don't let barking get out of hand. It's stressful for you and for your dog. Responding to the bark is part of controlling your dog's behavior and maintaining a calm environment. Barking alerts us to various happenings: another dog outside, an approaching thunderstorm, or someone at the door. Dogs do not bark for no reason. Ultimately, if you are responsive to her barking and her subtle communications, your dog will gain confidence knowing she is loved and safe.

Energy Communication

Dogs are aware of energy changes in the environment, even while resting. If you make a sudden move out of your chair, your dog will leap up and follow wherever you are going, even if it is only to the next room. Energy exchanges are a great way to express kindness and love. Rest your hand gently on your dog and let it remain in one spot until you feel the warmth of energy emanating from your hand and being received by your dog. This is a wonderful way to soothe and calm your dog.

What Dogs Hear

The Stare

If you have a dog or have been in a home that has a dog, you probably have experienced, *The Stare*. One of the most common reasons that dogs stare is because they want something. It's a very successful tactic as they are hard to ignore, and we eventually get up to satisfy their want. True dog training—yes, that is, we've been trained!

Just as humans stare into the eyes of someone they adore, dogs will stare at their owners to express affection. In fact, mutual staring between humans and dogs releases oxytocin, known as the love hormone. This chemical plays an important role in bonding and boosts feelings of love and trust.

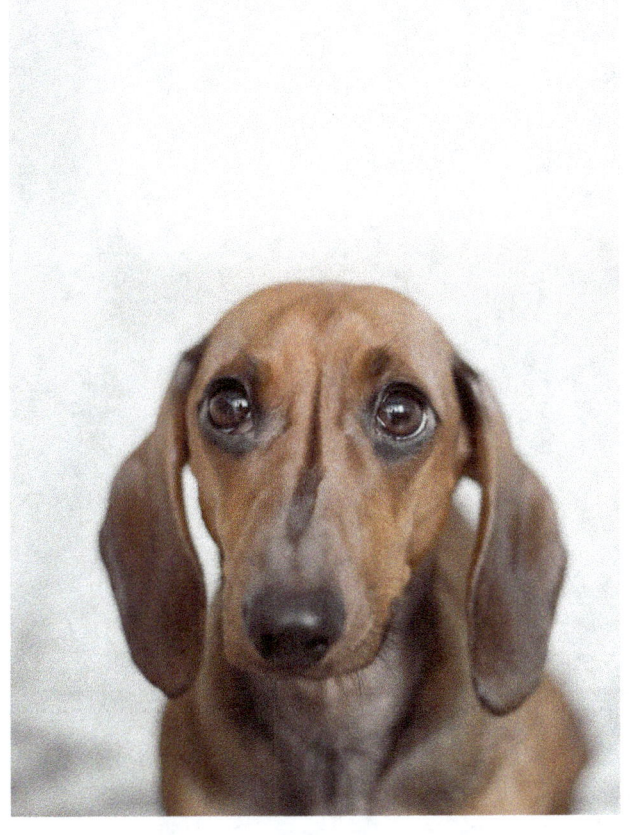

CHAPTER 12:

Mitigating Sound Stress in Shelters, Kennels, Homes, Veterinary Hospitals, and Training Environments

Shelters

Environments can be a positive or negative influence on canine behavior. You don't have to look further than shelters to find examples of high levels of stress, fear, and anxiety in dogs. Many dogs in shelters came from environments that created, or at least exacerbated, these behaviors. As soon as a volunteer comes into the kennel area for feeding or walks, dogs can be heard barking in varying states of need and stress. Thanks to these shelters and the good people who manage them, these animals have a temporary respite until a caring person or family brings them home. Shelters give us a vivid look at why animals need the feeling of connectedness and safety in their sonic environment. Helping the environment to be as calm as possible is key to mitigating stress.

The first step is to ask your team to walk around all the areas of the shelter with a decibel reader—especially in the dog kennel to measure the community barking—then convene to compare the list of spaces where decibels go above 80 dB. Measure the other sounds in the environment, such as washing machines, vacuum cleaners, door squeaks, visitors area, and slamming doors. With some practical fixes, sound can be mitigated. For example, placing a blanket over a washing machine can muffle the sound or put door stops to prevent doors from slamming. Acoustics panels on wheels can be moved to different areas of the shelter to mitigate noises. Many shelters broadcast music to help calm the atmosphere and mask the reverberations of barking.

My company, Pet Acoustics, consults with shelter administrators to help them mitigate their kennel environments. Sound reverberations are usually intensified because the walls are made from painted cement blocks. A good material for cleaning and harsh use, but, for sound, the walls become a reverberating canyon which enhances decibel levels to the extreme. It's a catch-22 for shelter environments.

Kennels

Several years ago, I was invited to see if I could help modify the kennel noise at the Fidelco Guide Dog Foundation in Bloomfield, Connecticut. This is an internationally recognized organization that breeds, raises, trains, and places German Shepherd guide dogs with individuals who are visually impaired. Lori McClain-Russak, Manager of Kennel Operations, coordinated with my team to begin a series of studies using our music speaker system approach. We were escorted into a large kennel area which had seventy German Shepherds in aisles of kennels. Lori opened the door and, because of our presence, all the dogs barked. The intensity of the sound was ninety-five decibels and above. You now know that is beyond canine and human hearing comfort. We were unable to hear each other talk until we closed the door to move back into the hallway. We saw what we needed to do. We returned a week later with a plan to place our music speakers in strategic spots that would have an acoustic expanse to calm the dogs in their kennels. Within two minutes of listening, the Shepherds were calmed and settling down to rest. The soothing environment spread to their neighboring kennelmates who also sat down and stopped barking. The Fidelco staff looked at us and smiled. You can see a video of the exact moment when this happened on our Pet Acoustics YouTube Channel: https://www.youtube.com/watch?v=PuuzrUEyh9A.

The next month, our team returned to Fidelco to outfit the whelping area, the training area and the rest of the kennels with speakers and frequency-modified canine music. At each stage of the two-year training program, this helped lessen the stress level in the kennel for the dogs. According to Lori, "This is important because the music helps them learn to relax because of what they are going to be doing, and that is to become guide dogs for the visually impaired."

Urban Apartments

Apartments pose a specific acoustic issue for dogs because you can't control sounds outside your home. It may be that, when you leave the apartment, your dog may spend his day waiting at the door for you to come home. Remaining in an alert state, your dog listens intently outside the door, hearing people walk in and out of elevators with floor vibrations absorbed by their paws and body. By the time you do get home, your dog has not truly rested and could be in stress mode from separation anxiety and noise stress. Perhaps you've observed that, as soon as you sit down, your dog will go into a deep rest near you to release his body tension back into balance because his person is now home. For apartment living, it's hard to avoid hallway and neighbor activity. Noise reactivity from a barking dog who might live down the hall or next door can also be a stressor for your own dog. If you are concerned that your dog is agitated from listening to a fur-neighbor's bark all day, I suggest installing a pet camera to see how long your dog actually naps in a day and to gauge the quality of rest. As mentioned before, sleep patterns are important to help balance your dog's health. I also suggest placing a music speaker on the floor by the front door to mask human voices, sounds, and movement.

Houses

For a dog at any age, your absence from the home can be a trigger for separation anxiety. Not only will your dog feel the pang of your absence, but she will also be responding to ongoing sounds inside and outside the home. Every dog needs her own bed to curl up in, maybe with a favorite stuffed toy or a special spot on the couch. Some dogs are left alone in silence. Generally, as a sound behaviorist, I recommend having some kind of sound in the air to distract from a sudden storm that can occur when you're not there to comfort your dog. In the development of canine-specific music, I have documented dogs that have listened to my pet music for many years with the same calming results. The music becomes the classical conditioning trigger for calm and rest.

What Dogs Hear

To minimize separation anxiety in your dog when you leave home, first make sure you're calm so you don't mirror your dog's anxiety, which can exacerbate her stress. Five minutes before you go, put music on and ask your dog to go to her bed or crate, and then let her know you'll see her in a little while. Keep your voice friendly, saying that you'll be going now. Your confidence will give her confidence. When you return, your dog should be happy to see you and ready for a walk.

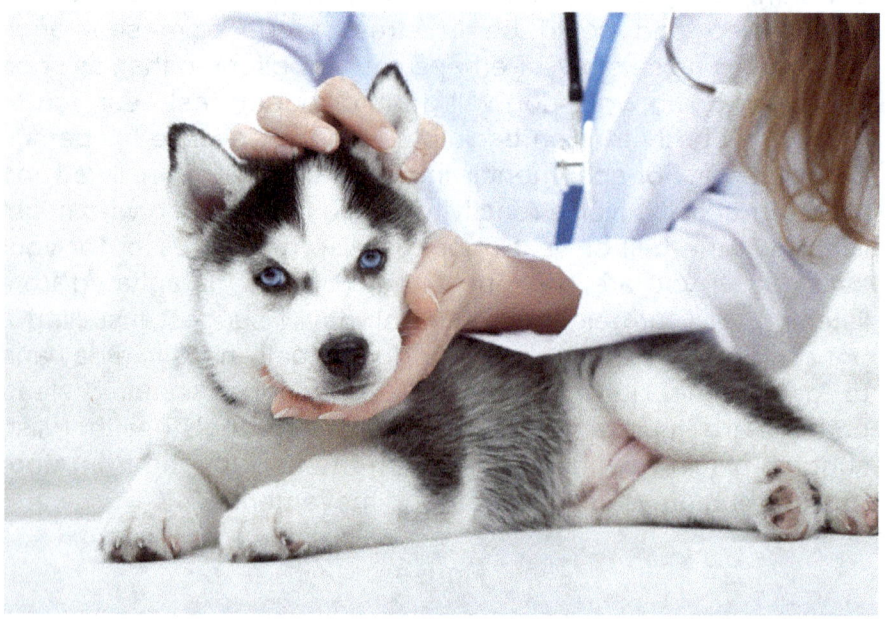

Veterinary Hospitals

There has been a significant movement in the past few years to modify the veterinary environment experience for dogs and cats to minimize fear and anxiety during health checkups and kennel stay overs. From the lobby, to the exam room, to the ICU and euthanasia room, many hospitals use calming species-specific music to modify anxious behaviors. Pheromones, lighting, and acoustic panels can also be used to help modify the hospital environment.

Service Dog Training

In 2018, I developed a study in collaboration with E.C.A.D—Educated Canines Assisting with Disabilities—whose training campus is located in Connecticut. E.C.A.D. provides highly skilled service dogs to increase mobility and independence for people living with disabilities, as well as veterans, children with autism, and for teaching facilities.

The study was set up to observe the benefits of introducing canine calming music to help dissipate the anxiety of both person and dog during two weeks of team training. The dogs are paired with their person right from the first moment they are introduced, which is stress-inducing for both. Our goal was to lessen the human-canine levels of stress during the team training by providing species-specific music during training sessions, dinner time, at sleep time, and during public training excursions.

After two weeks, the consensus from each team was that the dogs were:

- less hyper
- more relaxed and willing to train
- slept better
- calmer in their crate

Our clinical study questionnaire from the human members of the team stated overall that the music helped them feel calmer and more confident to bring their service dog home to begin a better life together. In the campus buildings of E.C.A.D., the music is played for each puppy litter and for everyday training and crate time.

Therapy Dog Training Environments

In 2010, my team and I collaborated with The Good Dog Foundation which is located in New York. A study was developed to evaluate the benefits of calming music used during their therapy dog training program. The Good Dog Foundation collaborates with researchers, healthcare professionals, and other organizations to promote research studies that document the effects of the human/animal bond for healing and wellness with therapy dogs. The study was implemented over a three-month period, collecting data via questionnaire and observation of fifty participants and their dogs. They attended obedience classes and learned therapy dog skills through The Good Dog Foundation. Participants were asked to be aware of their dogs at all times throughout each class and asked to report any findings they experienced with their dogs when the dogs were in the presence of the music speaker. Dogs and owners were also observed by the class instructor and class assistant for body language and stress signal changes that may have occurred. The human participants ranged in age from twelve years old to sixty years old, with an average of seven dogs in each class session. The canine participants were comprised of several different breeds of dogs as well as mixed breeds. All the dogs came from different backgrounds, including dogs from reputable breeders, animal shelters, humane societies, and rescue groups. The canine participants ranged in age from seven months old to ten years old. The mean and median age of the canine participants was three years old.

The findings of the study support the hypothesis that calming music played through the Pet Acoustics music speaker is beneficial not only to the canine participants, but the owners as well. The majority (75%) of human participants reported that the music relaxed them, while the remaining 25% of participants reported that the music was playing and enjoyable during the class session. Eighty percent of participants reported that they felt that the music calmed their dogs as well as themselves. Ninety-seven percent of participants felt that having the music in the room was a beneficial addition to the class atmosphere.

The majority of the canine participants (96%) displayed neutral to positive reactions as evidenced by their ability to focus on a task at hand with their owner. The canine participants displayed neutral body language and 86% of the dogs in the classes showed decreased frequency of stress signals and showed neutral to positive body language toward their owners. Four percent of canine participants showed elevated stress levels which were not compatible with the therapy dog program. Those dogs did not continue with the program.

CHAPTER 13:

Rhythms for 10,000 Walks

You may have seen some of the entertaining videos on social media of dogs singing in different pitched howls while their paws press the keys on a piano, elephants using their trunks to hold mallets while making melodies on a xylophone or a parrot singing and moving rhythmically while mimicking a Michael Jackson song. Animals respond to music because it has all the elements of language communication: volume (dB), pitch (Hz), and rhythm (beats).

Neuroscientists have proven that the power of music and sound affects our own human experience. It can lift our moods, lower levels of stress-related hormones (such as cortisol), and ease pain. Everywhere we go, we hear music. We hear music in stores, in restaurants, and in doctor's offices. Music is also tied to memories. A group of Dartmouth researchers has learned that the brain's auditory cortex, the part that handles information from your ears, stores music that we have heard as memories.

Walks

The power of sound is also a part of your dog's outside world, which you both share on your walks together.

Walking with your dog is one of the most beautiful and valued parts of your relationship because it is a time that balances you and your dog's partnership. A walk activates both human and canine senses while you share the fresh air, the exercise, and Nature. If a dog's life span is an average of fourteen years, you will walk your dog over 10,000 times!

Dogs look forward to walks with you whether on the road, on the city street, or on the nature trail. This is where your dog

What Dogs Hear

enjoys your company while happily activating his senses. When dogs walk, their most active senses are their noses and ears. When we walk, we are usually in our thoughts. A human has twelve thousand to sixty thousand thoughts a day. Dogs help us get out of our inner monologue of thoughts by perking up to a sound, catching a whiff of an interesting scent or stopping to analyze a foreign object. Taking a walk is an agreement between you and your dog and deepens companionship.

Since we take thousands of walks with our dogs, I'd like to offer a musical perspective while you walk together. Walks are truly like a musical composition. Walking together has phrasing, tempo, dynamics, and form.

- *Phrasing* has a beginning, a hi-point, and an end. There is always one interesting point in the middle of a walk, like meeting a friend and their dog for a conversation.
- *Tempo* is the pace at which you and your dog walk. Some days are energetic, and some days require a slower pace. Whatever your pace, your dog is aware of your energy level and will adjust to your tempo. You are partners in harmony.
- *Dynamics* are the volume levels experienced along the way. You may encounter a noisy construction zone or have a chance to pause for a quiet moment in a park—with an offered dog treat, of course.
- *Form* is the route that you take. In Native American folklore, it is said to complete a journey, instead of returning the same way, find a different route home to complete the circle.

Puppy Walks

When you teach your puppy to walk on the leash, make sure to use your voice along the way. Your puppy is imprinting the inflection of your voice to learn and understand your training communication. Keep your voice in a high pitch which is best for their high frequency hearing.

Establish a rhythm to your walk and keep your dog at that pace. As a simple training exercise, count a certain number of steps in a pattern and then stop to request a sit-stay. Repeat the counting pattern and then release into free-form walking, then go back to the pattern. Use puppy walks for training, socializing, and building confidence in creative ways.

Listening Walks

When we walk alongside our dogs, they are not only sniffing and seeing where they are going, but they are also hearing our footsteps. Tune in to hearing your own footsteps and then walk a little faster and watch your dog pick up the pace. Spend the walk listening to you and your dog's immediate surroundings.

What Dogs Hear

Dogs teach us to observe the path along the way. It is one of their greatest gifts to us as pet parents.

CHAPTER 14:

The Invention of Species-Specific Music

As I mentioned in the Preface, my life transitioned in 1994 from a recording and performance career to the study of animal hearing. *Species-specific* music is a term that I defined in 1997 when I produced my first music release on cassette for dogs and cats. By 1998, the music was transferred to a CD format and sold all over the world under the title, *Relaxation Music for Dogs and Cats*.

From 1994 to 1997, I solidified the formula of modifying frequency and decibel levels according to the hearing range of the animal in originally composed music. The frequency and decibel hearing range data that I based the music on was important because it helped me determine at what level sound triggers hypervigilance and stress. By creating a listening comfort zone, I could alter stress behaviors through music in an animal. This was and is still exciting work as I continue to underline that music is a powerful tool for animals just as it is for humans to effect positive change in behavior.

In addition to the sonic content of the music, the instrumentation itself required a parameter. Not all instruments are soothing for an animal. In my testing, long sustaining instruments, such as violins and flutes, offered the best results in dogs and cats, but brass instruments and percussion should be avoided. Maintaining a listening environment for the dog or cat by eliminating sudden volume changes, sharp tones, and fluctuations in frequency levels was a key component of the formula to elicit calm behavior. The results were measurable and repeatable.

Once I was underway with clinical studies proving the effectiveness of the canine and feline specific music, I moved on to equine music. My passion for horses has been a lifelong interest. In the studio, I developed frequency-modified music to elicit calm in horses for barn time, veterinary and farrier visits, trailer travel, and birthing. While studying equine behavior, my approach was completely different from what I used for canine and feline specific music, emphasizing, instead, the rhythmic gait of horses, composing music in 4/4 time, (walk) in 2/4 time, (trot), in 3/4 time, (canter and gallop). This worked well. One could see the horses moving in their stalls to the music, enjoy being ridden to the music, and being calmed by the music during grooming and massage sessions.

The equine music and speakers that I had developed were tested in a two-year study by Witold Kędzierski, Iwona Janczarek, Anna Stachurska, and Izabela Wilk through the Department of Biochemistry, University of Life Sciences, Department of Horse Breeding and Use, at the University of Lublin, Poland. This study tested one hundred and twenty purebred Arabian racehorses. The positive results showed that the horses who listened to the music won more races and were more relaxed. The study was published in the Journal of Equine Veterinary Science in 2015, *Music Calms Horses' Emotional State Study*.

A few years later, I received requests from owners of pet birds who shared behavioral issues, such as feather picking and depression from loneliness. The research on bird hearing is not as formulated in the scientific field as dog, cat, and horse hearing, but the need for music to elicit calm behavior is just as important. Birds are the most musical of animals. They need communication to establish behavioral balance as we care for them as pets. I composed soothing music and added sounds of nature and songs of other birds, such as Parakeets, Cockatiels, and Parrots, that the birds could call to and respond to. Through the years, anecdotal observable evidence have shown the avian music to be effective at modifying negative behaviors.

Through my association with a veterinary researcher in Santiago, Chile, Dr. Alicia Plaza Bobadilla, Director of Medvetarom, I was asked to create music for swine agricultural environments to study the effectiveness for behavior with music. I researched swine hearing and developed music for the study in 2016. The study was published in 2017 and entitled, *Evaluation of the Behavioral and Productive Effect of Music with Frequency-Modified Music in Piglets in a Commercial Production System* by Jimenez, MV 1., Plaza, A. 1, Sepulveda, D. 1, Acosta, J. 2 and Atlagich, M. 2 Zapata, B 1*, Universidad Mayor, Campus Huechurba, Rancagua Chile. The study concluded that the music contributed to the calming effect of the piglets and, thus, increasing their animal welfare.

I continue my collaborations globally with veterinary researchers to utilize species-specific music for the benefit of animals.

Baby Acoustics

When each of our sons were born, my husband and I would lean over their crib and sing two-part harmony Beatles' music and standard nursery songs to soothe them to sleep. Now, years later, I became interested in the study of infant and toddler hearing, as they have the same sensitivity to high frequencies as dogs and cats. "Babies are generalists and hear all frequencies simultaneously so they can respond to unexpected sounds," reports Lynne Werner, a UW professor of speech and hearing science, in the May edition of *The Journal of the Acoustical Society of America*. This statement piqued my curiosity, so I researched infant hearing, the use of white noise, and the range of dB levels best for baby sleep. I arranged classic nursery songs by modifying decibel and frequency levels accordingly. I also used real-sounding instruments, (no synthesizers) which is important for an infant's brain-ear development to identify sounds as they grow. The music is called *Baby Acoustics Sound Asleep*.

CHAPTER 15:

Follow the Dog

I hope the information in this book has enhanced your understanding of canine hearing and the importance of knowing how sound affects behavior. And, with this information, I hope you will gain continuous insights into the invisible world of your dog's hearing throughout her life. Our dogs are precious to us— and if we follow the trail of a dog into the human heart, we will surely have a better world.

ABOUT JANET MARLOW

Janet Marlow is internationally known as a composer, researcher, and author for her contributions to the understanding of animal hearing and how sound affects their behavior. Her research on behalf of animals has been featured on *Animal Planet*, *CNN*, *Good Morning America*, *The Today Show* and *The Wall Street Journal*.

For over two decades, Janet Marlow's passion for the understanding of the effect of sound on animal behavior has established her leadership in this new field. Her product innovations and media talks bring awareness to audiences into the complex world of animals.

Innovation

In 1997, Janet Marlow developed modified frequency and decibel music, the invention of species-specific music which results in calming behavior for dogs, cats, horses, and birds. In 2009, she founded Pet Acoustics, Inc. Today, Pet Acoustics' award-winning products have helped thousands of pets and pet parents, veterinarians, and shelters worldwide to solve stress-induced behaviors.

Awards

In 2017, Janet Marlow was named a Women of Influence in the Pet Industry by *Pet Age Magazine*. Fear Free Pets awarded her pet products as a preferred product recommended for veterinarians and pet parents. *Entrepreneur Magazine* named Pet Acoustics, Inc. "Top 100 Companies for Brilliant Ideas". She obtained a co-branding partnership with Nestlé Purina Friskies® from 2011- 2012, providing music and articles on feline behavior.

She is a member of the Animal Behavior Society, International Association of Animal Behavior Consultants, American Pet Product Association, and the Alliance of Therapy Dogs.

Author

Her books on pets include: *Zen Dog: Music and Massage for a Stress-Free Pet* (Barnes & Noble, Sterling Books), *The Magic of Music for Pets,* and *Dogs and Cats Hear Much, Much More!* (Amazon and Kindle).

Composer, Performer

Janet Marlow's roots in music come from a career as an international recording artist known for her mastery on the ten-string guitar. She has recorded jazz and classical albums. Janet is a fifth-generation musician from the Spivakowsky family of renowned artists.

Her performances have taken her around the world, which include venues such as the Lincoln Center, the Texaco Jazz Festival, Festival Estival De Paris, Quick Center for the Arts, The Apollo, Carnegie Hall, and the Blue Note. Her virtuosity has been heard as a soloist with orchestras and with her contemporary jazz quintet. She has composed for television documentaries, stage premieres in Hong Kong and Europe, and performs on screen in Woody Allen's movie, *Celebrity*. Her ten-string guitar playing is featured in the score of the Sundance award-winning film, *Swimmers*.

ABOUT PET ACOUSTICS

Pet Acoustics, Inc. is a global, award-winning brand founded by Janet Marlow in 2009 whose core mission is to innovate clinically-tested products that promote behavioral balance in dogs, cats, horses, and birds.

Featured Products

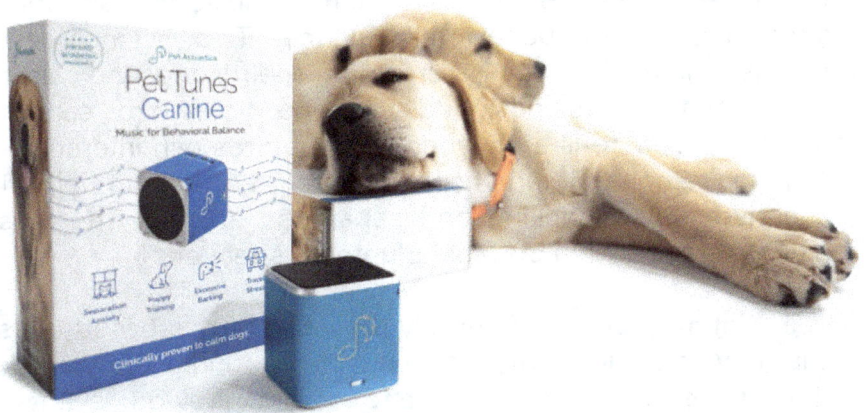

Pet Tunes Canine- Clinically-proven, science-based music designed for the sensitivity of your dog's ears. Canine specific music provides a listening environment that balances acute behaviors, such as separation anxiety, noise phobias, and excessive barking. Ideal for home-alone time, puppy crate-training, veterinary visits, travel, grooming, and adoption transitions. The music comes preloaded in a portable Bluetooth speaker.

What Dogs Hear

Pet Tunes Feline- Clinically-proven, science-based music designed for sensitive feline ears. This feline specific music provides a non-invasive solution to your cat's environmental stress, thunderstorm agitation, nocturnal activity or for adoption transitions. The music will help your cat modify stress behavior for crate travel, veterinary visits, grooming, and adoption transition. The music comes preloaded in a portable Bluetooth speaker.

Pet Tunes Equine- Clinically-proven science-based music designed for equine well-being. Calm your horse's behavior naturally with our scientifically-proven music designed to reduce stress. A solution for horse owners to modify equine behaviors during stall time, trailer travel, thunderstorms, veterinary visits, and grooming sessions. The music comes preloaded in a portable Bluetooth speaker.

Pet Tunes Avine- Birds are Nature's musicians and need communication for behavioral balance. This science-based music is ornamented with Nature sounds, birdsong, and calming instrumentation. It's designed to keep your bird calm by providing a Nature-like environment that birds can interact with when you're not at home. A solution for bird owners to help with excessive feather picking and separation anxiety. The music comes preloaded in a portable Bluetooth speaker.

Ultra Calmer Collar- Clinically-proven science-based music collar device designed for acute canine hearing. Help your dog ride out the anxiety of thunderstorms and firework events to other noise phobias with soothing music. At the first sign of agitation, snap on the collar and watch stress symptoms diminish as your dog settles into a state of relaxation. The collar also masks the intensity of thunder, lightning, and other frequencies that cause hypervigilant behaviors.

Fit Tunes Dogs- Science-based music based on the study of tempos of canine movement to stimulate more focus on your walking partnership. The music is preloaded into a clip-on Bluetooth speaker designed for a leash, belt or bag. Each lively track of varying tempos is ornamented with squeaky toys, whistles, human praises, and Nature sounds to keep your dog's ears perked to you and your walk. Observational studies show less pulling on the leash, less aggression toward other dogs, and less lunging at vehicles. Pairs with your smartphone to play other music.

Baby Acoustics Science-based music of classic nursery songs, designed for sensitive infant and toddler ears for sleep and nap time. Infant hearing is more sensitive than older children and adults. This music is modified for baby's ears to elicit calm for sleep. The music is preloaded in a plush bear toy with Bluetooth capability.

INDEX

Balcombe, Jonathan, 2, 5, 23
Bell, Alexander Graham, 4
Bioacoustics Research, 24
Cannon, Walter Bradford, 33
Coren, Stanley, Ph.D, 10
Cornell University, 24, 53
Dispenza, Dr. Joe, 6
Dodman, Nicholas, 59
Dog whistle, 41
E.C.A.D., 85, 109
Eyer, Joseph, 34
Fidelco Guide Dog Foundation, 5, 82
Galton, Francis, 41
Green Chimneys, ii
Haug, Lore, DVM, 63
Heffner, H.E., 5, 11, 20, 24
Heffner, R.S., 5, 11
Hertz, Heinrich, 5
Journal of Equine Veterinary Science, 98, 110
King, Barbara J., 23
Loew, Dr. Ellis. R., 53
MacKenzie, Liam, 58
Masteron, B., 110
Nappier, Dr. Michael T., DVM, DABVP, 30
North, Dr. Adrian, 58
Patterson-Kane, Emily, PhD, 18
Pavlov, Ivan Petrovich, 30
Payne , Katharine Boynton, 24
Radosta, Lisa, 64
Ratnayake, H.D., 30
Reby, David, Ph.D, 33
Ross, Dr. Samuel B., ii
Schumann Resonance, 6
Sterling, Peter, 34
The Good Dog Foundation, 5, 86

RESEARCH REFERENCES

Heffner, H.E. and Heffner, R.S. (2007) Hearing ranges of laboratory animals. Journal of the American Association for Laboratory Animal Science, 46, 11-13

Heffner, H.E. and Heffner, R.S. (1992) Auditory perception. In C. Phillips and D. Piggins (Eds.) Farm Animals and the Environment. (pp.159-184). Wallingford UK: CAB International

Masteron, B. and Diamond, I.T. (1973) Hearing: Central neural mechanisms. In: Carterette, E.C. and Friedman, M.P. (eds) Handbook of Perception, vol. 3 Biology of Perceptual Systems. Academic Press, New York, pp. 407-448

Music Calms Horses' Emotional State Study:

Stachurska, A., Janczarek, I., Wilk, I., and Kedzierski, W., 2015. Does music influence emotional state in race horses? Journal of Equine Veterinary Science, 35(5), 650-656.

Evaluation of the Behavioral and Productive Effect of Music with Frequency-Modified Music in Piglets in a Commercial Production System by Jimenez, MV 1., Plaza, A. 1, Sepulveda, D. 1, Acosta, J. 2 and Atlagich, M. 2 Zapata, B 1 *, Universidad Mayor, Campus Huechurba, Camino La Piramide 5750, Santiago Chile.

Heffner, H., Behavioral Neuroscience, 1983, Vol. 97, No. 2, 310-318

www.ingramcontent.com/pod-product-compliance
Lightning Source LLC
Chambersburg PA
CBHW071405290426
44108CB00014B/1697